Brother Francis

Brother Francis

AN ANTHOLOGY OF WRITINGS BY

AND ABOUT ST FRANCIS OF ASSISI

EDITED BY LAWRENCE CUNNINGHAM

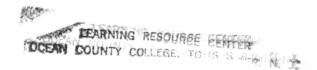
HARPER & ROW PUBLISHERS NEW YORK, EVANSTON, SAN FRANCISCO, LONDON

Acknowledgment is gratefully made to the following for permission to include copyrighted materials:

Cowles Communications, Inc. for "The Hippie Saint" by Joseph Roddy, in LOOK Magazine, April 20, 1971. Copyright © Cowles Communications, Inc. 1971.

Simon & Schuster, Inc. for selection from *Saint Francis* by Nikos Kazantzakis. Copyright © 1962 by Simon & Schuster, Inc. Reprinted by permission of the publisher.

The Viking Press, Inc. for the chapter from *The Fathers of the Western Church* by Robert Payne. Copyright © 1951 by Robert Payne. Reprinted by permission of The Viking Press, Inc.

A. P. Watt & Son for selection from *St. Francis of Assisi* by G. K. Chesterson. Permission also of Miss D. Collins, Doubleday, and Hodder & Stoughton.

Lynn White, Jr. for his article, "The Historical Roots of Our Ecological Crisis," in *Science*, March 10, 1967.

The World Publishing Company for selection from *The Medieval World* by Friedrich Heer, translated by Janet Sondheimer. Copyright © 1961 by George Weidenfeld & Nicolson Ltd. English translation Copyright © 1962 by George Weidenfeld & Nicolson Ltd.

Brother Francis: An Anthology of Writings by and about Saint Francis of Assisi. Copyright © 1972 by Lawrence Cunningham. All rights reserved. Printed in the United States of America. For information address Harper & Row, Publishers, Inc., 10 East 53rd Street, New York, N.Y. 10022. Published simultaneously in Canada by Fitzhenry & Whiteside Limited, Toronto.

FIRST EDITION

STANDARD BOOK NUMBER: 06–0616407–4

LIBRARY OF CONGRESS CATALOG CARD NUMBER: 72–78080

Designed by C. Linda Dingler

Contents

47213   v

Introduction

Just recently the editor of a national weekly magazine published an article on the life and significance of Saint Francis of Assisi entitled "The Hippie Saint."* The title was not only an engaging one but also one that called to mind certain obvious parallels between the medieval saint and the members of the present-day counterculture. Giovanni (nicknamed Francesco) Bernardone did come from a comfortable, upper-class family. He did have a terrible falling-out with his very straight businessman-father when he began to rebel against the comfortable life in which he had been raised. The upshot of that family quarrel was a new life-style for the young man which included unkempt clothes, a healthy disregard for conventional hygiene, a life of wandering, a refusal to get a decent job and settle down, and a vague yet determined idea that he could save the world by preaching a doctrine of love and forgiveness coupled with a plea to abandon the moneyed values of the well-to-do of society.

More significant than these admittedly superficial parallels between the more radical of today's youth and Francis of Assisi are the strikingly similar attitudes that both share on two very contemporary topics: the relation of man to his natural environment

---

*Symbol refers to articles or excerpts found in the anthology.

and the connection between personal happiness and the acquisi-
tion of material wealth. In both cases one finds a complete harmony of minds on the two topics. Both Saint Francis and the
"hippies" revere the world of nature and disdain the world of
wealth.

But, when all this has been said, the parallel between the two
begins to break down, or at least it needs to be modified. To
identify Francis as a medieval prototype of the "now" generation
is to simplify the image of a man who is infinitely more complex.
It is also to cloud over other facets of the personality and significance of a man who has a far wider right to the attention of our
own age.

The tendency to view Francis as a sort of charming, medieval
"nature freak" is a case in point. Ever since the last century, there
have been innumerable statues of Saint Francis with a dove
perched on his shoulders gracing innumerable gardens of believ-
ers and nonbelievers alike. The popular sentiment behind such
art is the idea that Francis is both a protector of nature and a
perfect example of a person who receives spiritual nourishment
from the world of nature. It is not a totally erroneous picture,
even if it is a bit sentimentalized. In fact, there are good reasons
for accepting such a picture of the saint once some careful distinctions have been made. Professor Lynn White in his now famous essay* and, much earlier, G. K. Chesterton* in his biography of the saint have provided such distinctions for us.

Francis did not divinize nature. He was not a pantheist; his
attitude toward nature was a far cry from the Wordsworthian "In
nature and the language of the sense the anchor of my purest
thoughts, the nurse, the guide, the guardian of my heart and soul
of all my moral being." Francis believed in a God who was the
creator of the world. Because this world was good, coming from
the hands of a good God, this handicraft of God not only was
good, but also spoke eloquently of its creator. The attitude of
Francis is that of the psalmist: "The heavens are telling the glory
of God; and the firmament proclaims his handiwork" (Ps. 19). It

was that primal conviction that every single part of nature is a pure gift from God and valuable in its own right that furnished Francis with his starting point. He appreciated a thing for what it was (this is not as banal as it first seems), and he accepted it for what it was. It was that essentially democratic vision of the world that Lynn White has pointed out as being so radical and so pregnant with promise for those who would like to value the world more than we have in the past. A perfectly charming example of Francis's ability to balance the world of nature with the world of divine mystery is to be found in an idea that he evidently cherished and expressed to his friends:

Many times we remember him saying that if he had a chance to speak to the emperor he would persuade him to pass a law obliging every person to scatter corn and other grain on the roads and in the fields outside of the towns on Christmas so that the birds, especially our sisters, the song birds, would have an extra ration. This would be done in honor of the Son of God because he was born poor and the Virgin had to lay him in a hay manger between an ox and a donkey. (*The Legend of the Three Companions,** Chap. LXXI)

This feeling for the real goodness of the world also helps to explain why the symbolic gesture plays such an important part in the whole life-style of the saint. Because the elements of nature such as fire and water are gifts from God (and not simply because they are symbols), they can be sung about as pointing to God. "The Canticle of Brother Sun,"* the earliest poem in the Italian language, is a hymn to God, not to the sun, but it is overflowing with the wonder of God's revelation in this world. Saint Francis set up the first Christmas crib outside of the town of Greccio because, as he tells us, he wanted to *see* the poverty and discomfort of the Christ child in a real and tangible way. In the last period of his life, while praying on Mount Alverna, Francis wished to *feel* concretely the suffering of Christ in His passion. The resulting phenomenon of the stigmata (cf. the essay by Jörgensen*) was a tangible expression of this desire.

In all of this, one sees that it is a very particular attitude that Francis had about the world about him. Chesterton, in his charmingly paradoxical way, has put it well in saying that, properly understood, Francis was not a lover of nature. He never even uses the word. What Francis loved were birds, flowers, fire, water, animals, and people. He was interested in the concrete: he loved men, not humanity; wolves, not wildlife; Christ, not Christianity.

Curiously enough, it is in his attitude toward nature that one must also seek out the basis for the Franciscan view of poverty.

The voluntary embracing of poverty was by no means a unique contribution of Francis to Christian spirituality. Hundreds of years before his time, monks deliberately sought out solitude in order to live a life of poverty and work. There is a tradition of abandonment of material goods in order to seek the goods of heaven that stretches all the way back to the early anchorites and desert hermits; they, in turn, found their inspiration from the New Testament. However, when one compares their style of renunciation with that of Francis, there is a significant difference. The earlier tradition sought to live the poverty of Christ by imitating his flight to the desert; Francis sought poverty in the milling crowds of the world. In other words, he desired to insert himself and his followers in the milieu of those who were the most abandoned of society. Francis dates his own conversion in his testament* to his meeting and embracing of a leprous beggar. We are perhaps too far removed to realize what courage it took in the Middle Ages to meet a leper, much less to embrace one, to understand how profound a change had come over the young man.

Saint Francis thirsted for Christian perfection, and in an attempt to assuage that thirst, he freely elected to live a life of total poverty. As Pope John XXIII commented, Francis wanted to possess God so completely, he was willing to give up everything else in the world. We must be very clear as to what that choice involved. It was not a simple desire to get back to a simpler form of living. It had nothing to do with a romantic attempt to rediscover the basic life-style of a less material-minded people. Nor was it merely a rejection of the comfortable life of his earlier days. These qualifications are added to prevent overly facile parallels with certain tendencies of our own time. To put the matter bluntly, one cannot make Francis a prototype critic of middle-class values simply because he wore ragged clothes, had long hair, had a beard, and went barefoot. He did in fact dress that way because the poor of his time neither could afford the barber, hope to own shoes, nor indulge in a new wardrobe. Saint Francis led a life of poverty, not merely a simple and plain life. That word *poverty* has been handled so loosely in our time that it has lost its real terrifying significance—except, of course, for the poor. In order to fully appreciate what Francis had chosen to do, one would have to imagine a latter-day Francis choosing to live, not a hand-to-mouth existence on the road, but a life that included rat-infested slums, the scanty medical care of our most inade-quate charity wards, long hours spent in the lines of the welfare bureau. In short, one would have to think of a man who had deliberately inserted himself in the terribly degrading apparatus of twentieth-century urban poverty. There was nothing romantic about this concept of voluntary poverty. Hunger, deprivation, cold, and misery, when fully experienced, simply are the stuff not of romance but of reality.

This deliberate choice of the poor life is intimately linked to his view of the natural world. Francis was not merely struck by the goodness of the world as it comes from the hand of God and is sanctified by the presence of God in the flesh of the person of Jesus Christ. For a man to freely choose the poorest of lives was, in a very real sense, to choose to imitate the example of God. It was to make an act of faith in the goodness of the created world and a willingness to attest to that faith by being an intimate part of it. Paul, in a famous passage in his letter to the Philippians, notes that Christ, while being the Son of God, did not think it an unworthy thing to "empty himself" and take on the form of a slave. So with Francis. He regarded it as a more complete follow-

ing of Christ to do the very same thing. He rejected the comfortable pleasure of the world in order to attest to the fact that the
whole world was good. He was such a lover of men that he wished
to be among those whom it is most hard to love. It was, to borrow
again from Professor White's felicitous phrase, the democratic
cast of his mind that caused him to preach the equality of men
by accepting the life of the least of men.

This deliberate choice of the poor life fit in well with Francis's
mission. He wished to preach Christianity, and he wanted to do
it in a way that would be most effective for the men of his own
time. He was not a social or religious *reformer* in any overt sense
of the term. He cannot be directly linked to that tradition of the
Middle Ages whereby individuals or groups grew to prominence
by reason or prophetic or apocalyptic preachments against the
ills of society or church. There is no instance in all of the records
of his life that he ever spoke as a conscious reformer. There is
abundant evidence that his very life was meant to be a sermon of
reform. Professor Heer's essay* quite rightly points out that the
life and actions of Francis had a rebuke and a word for many
segments of medieval culture: to the medieval Manichaeans, he
preached the goodness of the flesh and the material universe; to
the rulers, both secular and ecclesiastical, he pointed out that
Christ was not only a king but also a servant; to the warring
city-states, he reiterated the message of the Christian as peace-
maker; to the theologians and the prelates, he pointed to the
presence of God in the faces of the lowly. Yet all of this preaching
was accomplished more by his life than his words. Yet this
preaching by living example triggered something in the imagination of men. He started as a solitary, almost quixotic figure and
ended up as the inspirer of thousands of followers. He wished to
lead a hidden and simple life and found himself, even in his own
lifetime, lionized, venerated, and imitated. He also found himself
greatly misunderstood.

Earlier in this introduction, I took some pains to delineate just
how closely one could identify Francis as patron of the counter-

culture. This was not done with the fear that he would be appro-
priated by one segment of today's culture rather than another. I
rather suspect that in some ways Francis would be more comfortable in Drop City than on Wall Street. My intention was rather
to be fair to the man. Francis is a very easy person to misunder-
stand. If Joseph Roddy wanted to make him into a hippie, he was
merely one man in this century who wished to see him in a very
particularized light. At the turn of the century, Hermann Hesse
set up Francis as the ideal for the artist to follow. Nikos Kazantzakis* has tried to turn him into, well, Nikos Kazantzakis. Almost
every person who has been attracted by the man has been
tempted into seeing him as a sort of charming, romantic trouba-
dour who bumbled his way across the Umbrian countryside talking to animals like Doctor Doolittle and calling everyone *brother*
or *sister*. Behind all these stereotypes, there always lurks the grain
of truth. Francis was a singer, he did talk to animals, he did
believe in fraternity, he was a happy man. But that does not tell
his story. In fact, it falsifies it, albeit unwittingly. At the root of
this overromanticized vision of Francis is an instinctive unwilling-
ness to take him at face value. It is a problem in seeing the real
Francis today, and it was the source of much heartbreak for
Francis in his own time.

Toward the end of his life, Francis lost control of his own order
and, in the words of modern day management, he was "kicked
upstairs." In a process that began in the last years of his life and
greatly accelerated after his death, some very basic ideas of Saint
Francis (especially on poverty, the question of higher education
for his brothers, ecclesiastical privilege) had not only suffered
neglect but were ultimately modified or legislated against. There
were sporadic attempts to revive the ideals of Francis, but they
met with powerful resistance. Men who did attempt to revive
these earlier ideals, such as the spiritual Franciscans, were
harassed into untenable positions or persecuted out of existence.
The Franciscans became, in a relatively short time, a property
bound monastic group which, for whatever good the order did

do, bore little resemblance to the more or less unstructured life preached by Francis and his ealier followers. After the fourteenth century, the Franciscans were a creation more of Bonaventura than of Francis.

Paul Sabatier,* the man who initiated the revival of Franciscan studies in the last century, has attempted to explain this betrayal of the ideals of Francis as the conscious response of a highly juridical, clerically dominated and orientated, and essentially conservative ecclesiastical establishment (i.e. the medieval Catholic church) to an essentially lay, radical, democratic, and reforming movement that harbored within it, in their view, heretical elements that could well threaten its all-powerful hegemony over the minds and hearts of men.

Sabatier's thesis was so well argued that the Vatican put the book on the *Index,* but, despite the notoriety, his thesis is accepted by few scholars today. A much easier explanation is to be found in repeating what we have already said: his contemporaries had so romanticized Francis and his intention that, with rare exceptions, they could not really take him seriously. Francis wanted to live literally by some injunctions in the Gospel. Many of his followers found this idea of his to be overidealized, impractical, and romantic. His proposed mode of life could not answer such hard-nosed questions as, Who pays? How does one provide? What if? When Saint Francis answered such queries with "Our Father, who art in heaven," he was being serious. But it was only an answer that a saint would understand; to others, it was pious frivolity. What happened to Saint Francis in his time was what has happened to most charismatic religious leaders in history: his ideas became institutionalized and structured into law, because the followers lacked either the élan or the seriousness to keep the ideas alive with something approaching their original force. There is a bit more than sheer malice in Renan's quip that Jesus came preaching the kingdom of God and we ended up with the Catholic Church.

To avoid the romantic trap, it would seem then that the most rewarding approach for a contemporary understanding of Saint Francis is to be found in accepting him on his own terms, as a man of his own time, and then pointing out those elements of his life that can make continuing demands on contemporary attention. We must, in the last analysis, try to see why anyone beyond the medieval buff would be interested in a thirteenth-century saint. For it is my feeling that one must, in all fairness, emphasize that title of *saint* if one is to have a balanced and relevant view of the man.

Because of the romantic picture we have created about Francis, it comes as a bit of a shock to see just how much a creature he was of his own time; expecting to find poetry and metaphor constantly falling as dew from his lips, one has a sobering sense of disappointment on reading some of his prose. The admonitions,* while infused with the evangelical spirit of a man who believes in the power of the Gospel, nonetheless are less than satisfactory from the point of view of style. One marvels that the same man could have composed the soaring poem about Brother Sun and also written such dull and prosaic letters.

But the plain fact of the matter is that Francis was a medieval man. If his example and teachings transcend the period in which he lived, he nonetheless did live in that period. What is significant about Francis is that he was able to participate fully in the culture of his own time and yet stretch beyond it. He was a dutiful son of the medieval church, but he chastised it by his example and gave continuing hope to those outside of its pale. He submitted to the barbarities of medieval medicine, but, as Chesterton points out, he invested those moments with poetry. He believed in the whole tradition of medieval chivalry and transformed it into something far more substantive than the pretty *chansons* of Provence. In an age that brutalized or manipulated women, he exalted them and almost took them into partnership. As Nikos Kazantzakis* has so well intuited in his fictional recreation of the meeting of Francis and Clare, their relationship was based on that bold love of equals in common search for the Ultimate in love. There was something terribly unconscious in the way that Francis could cross genders; in his rule for hermitages,* the brothers become mothers and play at what we would call today "role reversal," while, at the same time, he could refer to one of his closest female friends as *brother*.

Yet it was in his search for God that Francis was so distinctively a child of his own time. The Middle Ages put a high premium on sanctity, and Francis sought that sanctity with unswerving devotion. The early legends of his life (such as the *Fioretti**) had no other intention than to exalt him as a searcher for complete identification with the person of Christ. Even the polemical slant of the legends (to bolster fidelity to the original ideals of the saint) were written to show that men should follow the example of man close to God. If Francis spoke to the animals, it was because he was in tune with the whole of God's creation. If Francis lived with lepers, it was because he had the supernatural strength to do it. If men were converted or cried tears of repentance or sold their goods and gave it to the poor—it was because Francis was a saint. The point is that his medieval chroniclers and followers saw him in that light. He had no other claim on their allegiance: he was not a graceful writer or a spellbinding preacher or an artist. He was a poor, ragged man who led the life of a hobo. But he was a saint.

The moot point is, of course, whether that same enthusiasm that his contempories had for the man can carry over today. Saints seem to be less marketable in our own time than in the past. This is especially true of saints who have had visions, had mystical experiences, preached fidelity to an organized religion, and generally behaved in a nonmodern way.

One possibility for the apologist of Francis (and I am an unabashed apologist for him) is to sanitize his image for modern man by demythologizing all of the manifestations of the medieval. This is not only a difficult task but also a destructive one. It would mean at the offset chucking out all of the art, legend, and fact concerning the man. It would mean hiding a good portion of what appears in these pages. Ultimately, it would mean to falsify.

A less-draconian approach to a contemporary understanding of Francis would be to understand Francis in terms of his own background, recognizing those elements in his life that are peculiar to his own culture, and then asking what other elements escape the medieval moment so as to speak to our own time. The merit of such an approach is that one can retain the charm of the legendary Francis without losing the genuine claim that he can make for our time.

What is the source of Francis's importance for our time? Offhand, I would say that it is to be found in his seriousness. This may appear to be paradoxical at first glance, since he seems to be such a lighthearted, whimsical, and essentially gentle person. But this only tells part of the story. There was another side of Francis that was totally dedicated, unbending, searching for the ultimate meaning of love and service, a God-haunted man who gave up all to obtain all. This seriousness changed him from the wealthy man of a comfortable Umbrian home to the blind, ragged figure of Mount Alverna. It was his seriousness about the reality and truth of what he read in the Gospel that turned his life into what it was. When Francis worked with his hands, sheltered outcasts, kissed a leper, or became a poor wanderer, it was because he had a model for this behavior. Poverty for him was not an affectation; nor was it a protest. It was an imitation of the One who shed the glory of heaven for the slavery of human existence.

My thesis then would be that the contemporary relevance of Francis is to be found precisely in this utter seriousness. This seriousness, it turn, speaks to men of our time in slightly different ways. It says one thing to those who come to Francis with some commitment to Christianity and something else to those who do not.

To men in the church, the figure of Saint Francis is an embarrassing one. He keeps the Christian a bit off guard, because his life is a totally serious attempt to answer the question that the Gospel itself asks: What think ye of the Christ? The person of

Saint Francis, in all of its manifold manifestations, does not permit a facile answer to that question. Francis is, in the deepest biblical sense of the word, a *reproach* to those who would like to make Christianity over by restructuring either their lives or their institutions in a peripheral or tangential manner. The life of Francis compels those who would rearrange rubrics, reshuffle administrative bodies, or form committees to ask whether that type of reform will move men to kiss the outcasts of today, to confront poverty in an open and loving way, to bless peace and tame the wolf of war and strife. No Christian can read the *Fioretti* and evade the question of whether perfect joy is to be found in the cross, just as no Christian can read Jörgensen's account of the stigmata of the saint and avoid the "scandal" of the cross. No Christian, in short, can ask for the meek Francis without asking about the suffering one; for both sides of this one man are reflections of the One whom he hoped to imitate. Someone once wrote that Christianity has not been tried and found wanting; it simply has not been tried. Francis tried Christ and was not disappointed. That is the whole point of his life.

If Saint Francis can serve as a "reproach" to the Christian, he can also serve as a challenge to the non-Christian and to the unbeliever. For the life of Saint Francis raises an interesting question. It is a question that is not totally disengaged from the question of the credibility of the truth claims of Christianity, but, at the same time, it is one that can be raised somewhat independently of them. Saint Francis led a life that had many attractive qualities—qualities that are much envied today. He was a man profoundly concerned with peace among men; he was passionately dedicated to the fraternity of the rich and the poor; he was totally compassionate to the suffering of the dispossessed of this earth; he was profoundly reverential toward the beauty of this earth. He was a man who risked all for love. All of these facets of his life find familiar resonance in the strivings of sensitive persons today. We are all concerned with the quality of life on our planet, as we are concerned with the racial and class conflicts that tear at the very fabric of civilized life. There are also evident signs in our culture, especially among the young, that the thrist for a sense of the transcendental has not been quenched by the rush of our post-Enlightenment culture.

In the face of such challenges and problems, one is forced to ask if there is not a crying need for the seriousness that was so clearly evident in the life of Francis. The life of Francis of Assisi forces the question of whether individuals and societies can afford to live without totally serious men in their midst to sort out the way. His life in fact brings up the whole embarrassing question of whether we can really live humanly and creatively without saints.

In the life of this man, as we discern it in the writings by and about him, there are elements that belong to neither his own age nor ours; they are rather questions about life itself, for they deal with the very texture of human existence: life and love, suffering and death, beauty and ugliness, gentleness and fierceness, poetry and prayer. In a very real sense, to look back to medieval Umbria is to see ourselves in our aspirations and in our strivings. It is worth a look.

*   *   *

A word about this anthology: This book does not pretend to be a definitive statement about the life of Saint Francis, nor does it hope to present a single idea about his message. It could best be likened to a mosaic in which different pieces of writing, ranging from medieval texts and legends to contemporary essays, sermons, and selections of fiction, are grouped in sections with the hope that what will emerge is a coherent picture of some of the more striking themes of the most beloved of Christian saints. Like a mosaic, and very unlike oil painting, only the main lines will emerge. The subtle variations are to be filled in by the spectator. This is totally consistent with the ideals of Francis himself. He conceived of his life as a faint mirror of his master. He wanted people to see beyond him to the person of Christ; his love and happiness were meant only to reflect the love of God. People were to see through him to Christ.

This anthology then hopes to be a first word about a man who loved this world, the men in it, and the God over it with a singular intensity. It is hoped that some of this love for the fullness of life will shine through these writings by the saint and his most faithful interpreters.

The translations from the writings of Saint Francis, from the *Fioretti,* and from the work of Sabatier have all been done by the editor. There has been no attempt to create a literal fidelity to the original text. The translation from the Latin writings is based on the *Opuscula Sancti Francisci Assisiensis* (Quaracchi, 1904); the text of "The Canticle of Brother Sun" is from *Gli Scritti di San Francesco d'Assisi* edited by Vittorino Facchinetti (Milano, 1967). I have also used Monsignor Facchinetti's notes to good advantage. The selections from the *Fioretti* are based on the Einaudi edition edited by Guido Divico Bonino (Torino, 1968).

My thanks are due to any number of persons for their aid and encouragement. My special devotion is here expressed to CJD, who believed in the work and encouraged it. To her my labors are dedicated with love.

FRANCIS OF ASSISI

PART ONE

Francis of Assisi: Some Interpretations

Francis of Assisi: The Hippie Saint

"Your way of living without owning anything," the bishop of Assisi said to Francis, "seems to me very harsh and difficult."

"My Lord," Francis answered, "if we possessed property, we should need arms to defend it."

No revelation that. There were always arms for the propertied, bishops for defense, and no end to the harshness and difficulties around the unpossessing. Yet there stands the scruffy little Umbrian figure of Francis di Bernardone out of that unfashionable thirteen century, a bearded, barefoot, slightly prankish and largely unfathomable man, but a man the world now in torment finds more alluring every day.

It is an allure that can escape purpled bishops and the heavily propertied, to be sure, though they honor him with insipid statuary in birdbaths, ply children with pretty tales of his chats with beasts and exclaim over the success of the religious society he started for medicants, who now manage real estate worth maybe more than all the the city of Assisi.

It was the success-mongers in medieval Assisi who hustled the first Franciscan into official sainthood two years after he died in 1226. Even then, canonization was a deft way to isolate and have

Joseph Roddy, "The Hippie Saint," *Look*, April 20, 1971, pp. 32–37.

3

done with anyone whose imitation of Christ embarrassed practical Christians. "The Lord told me to become a new type of simpleton," Francis was saying while the first organization men were bringing practicality, efficiency and common sense to his band of gentle vagrants.

They were the medieval precedents for his latter-day crowd hailing from the hippie communes, the unchurchable young discovering that owners are themselves fatally owned. The faith of these new Franciscans—like the first Christians—is in a counterculture. Their hopes are that the world will turn truly communal fast or the very roof of heaven will fall in.

What a friend they have in Francis. He was the son of a rich man in dry goods, and right from the start he was a trouble to his father. When his son was born, Pietro di Bernardone was in France going about his fabrics. By the time he made it back to Assisi, it was to find that his French wife had already named their infant John. The father would not have it, and renamed the boy Francis, to get him started out right in life as the courtly young French-type man the upward-bound Umbrian planned to have his son be. From the town priests, Francis learned little. But from Assisi's young sports, the youth learned to sing, drink, dance, wench and, that the first few times around, a little revelry is not quite the vast repugnance the parish priests made it out to be.

When Perugia went to war against Assisi, 20-year-old Francis was taken prisoner, and by all accounts found jail a good place to get on with his singing. His taste for the fleshpots slackened there, and once out, he found himself instead listening for a guiding voice of the force Saul heard on the road to Damascus, the voice Joan was to hear at the siege of Orléans. "All that which now seems to you sweet and lovely will become intolerable and bitter," was what it said. "But all which you used to avoid will turn itself to great sweetness and exceeding joy." On the road before him then was a leper, abhorrent to see, foul to smell, but with hands to be kissed, and Francis kissed them. Not only kissed them but pressed money into them—money that had lost its savor for him, though it was mostly not his, or almost entirely his father's. When that voice he listened for told him that the chapel of San Damiano near Assisi needed restoring, young Di Bernardone acted. Ne went back to his father's shop, loaded his horse with bolts of fine cloth and rode off to the next town, where he sold the cloth and the horse and gave all he got for them to the old priest sitting in the sun outside San Damiano. Francis was back in the cave he had taken to living and meditating in when the senior Di Bernardone noticed the loss and hauled his son into the bishop's court. "My Lord," said the accused, "I will not only give him the money cheerfully but also the clothes I have received from him." In a moment, Francis had them all off, had his father disowned and faced a very unencumbered future. When he left the bishop's house, he was wearing the old cloak the gardener had discarded, and when he had fitted himself with a beggar's bowl, he had just about all he needed then to be a Franciscan.

All accounts make him out to be the merriest of mendicants, but a mystic whose overpowering faith compelled other men to follow him. First came two, giving away all they owned, then four more, then by the dozens, and then came the rock-solid Assisians who were offended by the odd ways of the beggars Francis called Friars Minor. "Many men took the friars for knaves or madmen and refused to receive them into their houses for fear of being robbed," three followers then living with Francis wrote. "So in many places, after having undergone all sorts of bad usage, they could find no other refuge for the night than the porticos of churches or houses. . . .

"There were those who threw mud upon them, others who put dice into their hands and invited them to play, and others clutching them by the cowl made them drag them along thus. But seeing that the friars were always full of joy in the midst of their tribulations, that they neither received nor carried money, and that by their love for one another they made themselves known as true disciples of the Lord, many of them felt themselves reproved in their hearts and came asking pardon for the offenses which they had committed. They, pardoning them with all their heart, said, 'The Lord forgive you' and gave them pious counsels for the salvation of their souls."

They were so burgeoning a band in 1210 that Francis and 12 friars went to the Vatican to establish themselves as a religious society. The Pope, Innocent III, thought their way of life too severe, but since all they sought was the right to live as Christ had, to deny them would be to deny that following the gospel was possible.

Francis was not a priest, nor were his first friars, but their audience with the Pope started them down the road to absorption. Paul Sabatier's biography of Francis, a work the Franciscans even now do not quite cherish, laments that agreement. As a result of it, "the thoroughly lay creation of St. Francis," Sabatier writes, "had become, in spite of himself, an ecclesiastical institution: it must soon degenerate into a clerical institution. All unawares, the Franciscan movement had been unfaithful to its origin."

Others thought it foundered over the figure of Clara Sciffi, the devout daughter of a noble family in Assisi. She was 16 when she heard Francis preach and came at once to the view that she too would have to be one of his missionary troupe. By simply ignoring canon law, Francis decided that could be arranged; and late on Palm Sunday night in the year 1212, she was the first woman accepted into his society. The friars had just finished singing matins when Francis himself cut off most of her hair. In place of her shining dress, he decked her out in a black veil, a coarse woolen robe, and a knotted rope to bind it at her waist. That night he took her to live with Benedictine nuns a few miles away, where her outraged father found her but could not induce her to return home. Like Di Bernardone, Sciffi was another status quo parent sure to go unnoticed in Assisi had it not been for a rebellious child. Clara's younger sister joined her in a week, followed later by their youngest sister, then by their widowed mother.

The lady Franciscans, known now as the Poor Clares, lived

then at San Damiano, a few miles away from the Porziuncola, the ten-foot-long chapel still there as the birth-house of the Franciscans. Francis seldom preached at San Damiano, but pious tradition has him under the olive trees and in the care of Sister Clare with his sight nearly gone when he wrote and sang The Canticle to the Sun. It is among the few perfect hymns of praise that are also exalted acts of faith.

Before that, Francis was given to leaving Assisi for spells of solitary contemplation and to spread his beliefs. If he loved the birds and talked with them, it was also to tell them to be quiet while he preached. He was particularly forthright in telling a wolf in the town of Gubbio, that he had to mend his ways, and that once his attacks stopped, the townsfolk would see to his care and proper feeding. He called his own body, but not without courtesy, Brother Ass. That was the brother he never subdued to his satisfaction, and he knew he had lost to that beast once more the night he found himself eating a chicken after preaching fasting and abstinence to Umbrians. The next day he had another friar lead him through the town on a halter. "Look here, you people," Francis called out as he passed, "this is the man who asks you to fast and repent while he himself feasts on a tender bird just because his stomach hurts him a little. That glutton, that reveler, that hypocrite!" He turned up at fine dinners in episcopal palaces with his beggar's bowl. He threw money he was owed into dung heaps. And his first time in Rome, Francis was so poorly turned out when he bowed to Innocent III that the offended Pope said he should go and roll in a pigsty. Francis did, the biographers say, then returned even more redolent for his audience in the Vatican. He was the pure fool for his faith, the hard-line follower of Christ, and just maybe the precursor of Chaplin.

He was never more the man for his God, inseparable from pathos, than when he set out to convert the Moslems in Egypt while the Christian armies of the Crusade were drawn up outside Damietta to massacre them. Ministering to the Crusaders was disheartening even to Francis, for all about him he saw the Pope's legions steadily gluttonous, drunk and dissolute. Harlots from Sicily were circulating through the tents with all manner of relic hawkers following, and when the lucre was gone from the sacred coffers, blessed suits of armor were sold off to pay painted ladies or bartered for more pieces of a true Cross. Appalled by the Christians, Francis was conducted through the battle lines to bring the Word of God to the Moslems he thought heathens. Their sultan, Maliak-el-Kamel, in perfect civility, heard the sermons about a creed he found strange but not compelling. When the Saint had given up on him, the Sultan saw him safely back to his fellow-believers. Francis continued on quickly to Assisi.

The trouble back in Italy was the trouble most saviors have with their disciples. There were thousands of Franciscans by then —men, women and near-children, each devout in some fashion and all certain about the form their devotion took. When the Friars Minor were just a ragtag few, their begging and vagrancy were more quaint than disruptive. But beggar packs on the streets and crowds of men without homes seemed a threat to public order. Yet the larger problem was within the Order itself. Francis was always to be the society's spiritual leader, but he found it beyond his talents to be its administering general too. Although he had never expected it of them, his Friars Minor had grown into an organization. Its administrators in Assisi were finding that most discontent stemmed from the vow of poverty that all new disciples found easy to make but arduous to observe. Ownership was not the only problem. There were friars who wanted to change his rules on fasting and abstinence. Another, with ambitions for a splinter movement, petitioned the Pope to let him found a new society to care for lepers. In Bologna, the Franciscans were putting up a fine house of studies for themselves. Francis had forbidden them to carry anything, and now they were even planning to carry books. "There are so many in our days who want to seek wisdom and learning," he said, "that happy is he who out of love for the Lord our God makes himself ignorant." Learning was of little worth in Francis' view, but his growing society was growing its own theologians, then canon lawyers, as well as ambitious ecclesiastics who wanted dioceses, red hats, offices in the Roman Curia and maybe the Throne of Peter itself. It was enough to make the poor Saint want to start all over again, but it was too late.

A faint aura of authority still clustered about their spiritual leader, but through their ministers-general, the Franciscans came under the firm rule of Rome. To resist that would have taken administrative strength, and what little of that Francis ever had was long gone. "Where are they who have ravished my brethren from me?" he cried out one day. "Where are they who have stolen away my family?" And his Brother Ass was spent too. He suffered from hemorrhages and from stomach infections, and when thirteenth-century healers tried saving his eyesight by cauterizing his temples he showed fear. "Brother fire," he said as the irons were brought to him, "be favorable to me in this hour; you know how much I have always loved you." But it was not favorable, and the treatment left him as before but now hideously burned. Then came the wounds in his hands and feet, thought to be stigmata matching the wounds of Christ. When his own death was so plainly near in the fall of 1226, his closest followers brought him in a litter to the tiny Porziuncola. He was there, singing his Canticle to the Sun in a whisper the day before the life went out of him.

He left a will charging his friars to resist change and stay simple and poor, but in no time at all, it was burned to ash over the head of a friar who wanted to live by it. Gregory IX, the Pope who made being a Franciscan much easier than Francis ever had, caused a great basilica to rise up in Assisi to honor the Saint. Visitors are quick to compare it to the tiny Porziuncola, and they know then how the truth of the Saint can make the mighty despair.

Saint Francis: The Medieval Man and His Culture

And so we have come to Assisi, where, in 1204, the star of St. Francis was already in the ascendant. This saint of the Catholic Church, venerated by his much-harried and devoted companions as the "second Christ," has won friends and admirers far outside his own Church and time; the power radiating from the Poverello has touched many different kinds of men and women, including the reformers of Luther's day, non-conformists of the eighteenth and later centuries, and people right outside Christendom. We may wonder whether it was merely by accident that the earliest writings about him, the testimony of his earliest and closest companions, were rediscovered only at the close of the nineteenth century. It may also be significant that they were found in the archives of Poor Clares, Franciscan nuns, where they had been deposited to save them from destruction. And is it an accident that it is only now that Franciscan studies are sufficiently advanced to permit us to strip away the layer upon layer of false piety and sentimentality, sometimes deliberately superimposed, as in many early Christian paintings in the catacombs, so that the

From Friedrich Heer, *The Medieval World,* (New York: Mentor Books, 1962), pp. 222-32.

features which begin to emerge at last bear some resemblance to the reality?

Thomas of Celano's account of the saint's physical appearance is confirmed by the earliest portraits, still free of the idealization found in later paintings: the fresco in the Sacro Speco at Subiaco, the portrait behind the choir of San Francesco a Ripa at Rome, and parts of the Franciscan cycle of Bonaventura Berlinghieri at San Francesco, Pescia.

"In stature he was rather on the short side, his head of moderate size and round, his face long and thrusting forward, his forehead smooth and low, his eyes of medium size, black and candid, his hair dark, his eyebrows straight, his nose even-shaped, thin and straight, his ears prominent but delicate, his temples unfurrowed. In conversation he was agreeable, ardent and penetrating, his voice firm, sweet-toned and clearly audible, his teeth were white, even and close together, his lips delicate, his beard black and rather sparse, his neck slender, his shoulders straight, his arms short, his hands small, with long fingers and narrow nails, his legs thin, his feet small, his skin tender, his flesh meagre, his clothing rough, his sleep brief and his bounty most liberal."

The portrait is clear and precise, free of any suggestion of sickly suffering. In 1260-63 the General Chapter of the Franciscan Order commissioned its Minister-General, Giovanni da Fidanza, otherwise known as Bonaventura, to compose an official life of St. Francis. After it appeared an attempt was made to track down and destroy all biographical writings emanating from the saint's personal circle.

Neither Celàno nor Bonaventura reveals to us the authentic saint, the man who radiated both joy and sorrow, who united serenity and grief, quietude and turbulence, who rejoiced in all men, animals and things, yet was austere with the fortitude of the Desert Fathers, whose spirit was born of love out of fire, whose countenance was veiled in blood and tears: a man crucified. The appearance on Francis's body of the stigmata, the wounds of Christ, is the first recorded instance of this phenomenon among

Christians of the West. The Eastern Church knew nothing of such
miracles and had no wish to know them. Christ's Passion was not
much dwelt upon in Eastern Christendom. What counted there
was his Transfiguration; Christ was the lord of the cosmos; He
was caught up as a man with the circle of light radiating from the
triple sun of the Godhead which shed on man its benign radiance.
This was the teaching about the humanity of Christ current in the
Eastern Church.

But God became man, and wholly man, born a naked infant
and laid in the manger. Francis set up his Crib at Greccio not as
a pretty toy but to be a dread and solemn warning to the mighty,
to theologians and to ordinary Christians: "Behold your God, a
poor and helpless child, the ox and the ass beside Him. Your God
is of your flesh, He lives in your nearest neighbour, in every man,
for all men are your brothers."

The Crib, the stigmata, the preachings to the beasts, St. Francis's whole life of dedication to his bride, Lady Poverty, were all
messages addressed to those great powers who in this fateful
hour were struggling in Italy and Europe for the possession of
mankind. To the Cathars the message ran: God is not only "pure
spirit" but also wholly man, vulnerable, helpless, bleeding flesh,
the blood of brother men, too precious to be shed in warfare of
any kind. To Byzantium and the Eastern Church it said: even in
his Transfiguration, Christ still appears to us poor men in His
crucified body (Francis's vision on Mount La Verna). To Rome,
the Church which claimed to rule the emperors and kings of this
world, it said: Christ came to earth to be the servant of His own.
The war-mad Italian towns, standing for embattled Christendom
as a whole, were reminded that Christians were called to be
peacemakers. Francis brought the wolf into the town as his
brother. *Homo homini lupus,* man is as a wolf to other men; such
was the pessimistic wisdom of antiquity, and the political "real-
ism" of rulers and governments in the Middle Ages. Francis, who
preached to the animals and made friends with "brother wolf,"
dissented from this view, protesting that all creatures and all men

were created by God to be brothers.

But it would be quite wrong to describe the Catholic saint as any kind of "protestant." A protestant protests against something. Francis was "against" nothing. The "poor little Francis" was not found preaching against Cathars and Waldensians, although he knew very well what they were. Nor did he preach against the Emperor and the imperial party in Italy, just entering on their last great struggle with the Papacy at the time when Francis was at his most influential. Francis was also a silent witness of the conflict between Assisi and the Pope in 1204, as already mentioned; in fact he had just returned to Assisi from Perugia, where he had been imprisoned for his part in the war between Perugia and Assisi. Nor did he preach against the Pope, but rather submitted himself wholly to him, to his own bishop and to all priests. Francis the layman (he had only minor orders and never became a priest) declared his continuing faith in priests in his Testament: "If they should persecute me, I would yet wish to have recourse to them." Francis knew no "against," no boundaries; he was as ingenuous with the Sultan as with his brethren in Italy.

Francis taught the good news for what it was: a message of joy and love, God dwelling at peace with men, mediated by Christ to his brother men. His experience of the being of Christ was something concrete, a historical fact. Contemporary medieval society, whose daily life was warfare, unrest, tumult, hatred, envy and the lust for power, all those sinister beasts of prey whom Dante saw stalking through the world, was confronted with its greatest challenge. Francis knew that in such a world an open heart meant a heart ready to accept the world in its entirety, to transform it by a life of unsullied sacrifice. "Toleration" meant for Francis what it had meant for Paul and Christ: submission to the death of the Cross, and before that a life spent until its last hour in bearing the cross of this world.

Giovanni Bernardone was born in 1181 or 1182 at Assisi, the son of Pietro Bernardone, a wealthy cloth merchant whose business took him frequently to the south of France; he was, it seems, attending a trade fair there when Giovanni was born, and on his return gave his infant son the additional name of Francesco, in honour of the sweet South. Francis's mother may have been French, a native of Picardy. Francis's youth was like that of any rich young man in a wealthy and licentious town. It was a spell of illness and imprisonment that released his particular genius for seeing all things as though for the first time through the eyes of the Creator, and revealed to him that his first duty was to cultivate a serene self-detachment from everything rooted in warfare and the perpetual commotion of the city; in fact from envy and hatred. "Listen everyone and understand it well: until now I have called Pietro Bernardone my father; but now that I intend to serve the Lord I am returning to this man all the money which has caused him such a bother and all the clothes that were his property; and from now on I shall say Our Father which art in Heaven, instead of my father, Pietro Bernardone."

The world was cheerfully abandoned that the world might be served; Francis took to the road in complete poverty, earning his daily bread by the labour of his hands or by begging, and as he went, he preached. He has himself summarized the substance of his message: "Fear and honour God, praise and give thanks to Him . . . Father, Son and Holy Ghost. . . . Do penance . . . for you know that we must soon die . . . Confess all your sins. . . . Blessed are those who die penitent, for they will be in the Kingdom of Heaven, while the unconfessed . . . will go to the everlasting fire. Guard yourselves from all evil and persevere in goodness till the end."

Francis was not thinking of founding an Order. With his brethren he begged and preached his way through Italy, southern France and Spain. The people flocked to him, seeking peace and joy, seeking a new image of God and a new brotherhood.

What was it that distinguished these "penitents from Assisi" as they called themselves, all of them laymen, from the sundry heretics, hotheads, "Poor Men of Christ," Humiliati, Waldensians and Albigensians who also thronged the roads of south-western Europe, preaching where they could? One main difference was that Francis was persuaded of the need for papal approval and a Rule if his brotherhood was to escape being swept away in the wake of persecution. Heretics menaced by this danger, particularly Waldensians, were quick to seek shelter under the wing of the new community, which grew at a fantastic rate; by 1282 the Franciscan Order possessed 1,583 houses in Europe. But Francis himself desired no "house," no safe stronghold, no cloister, no possessions, no privileges: all these things he saw as fetters, links with the affairs of the world. His brotherhood was to be defenceless, exposed. He forbade the brethren to go to the Pope for letters of protection and privileges. Christ's friends and disciples on earth should remain in complete poverty, without possessions and without legal protection. Such complete abnegation created a new kind of asceticism, a new appreciation of the world, a new kind of joy: serene and unencumbered, the friend of holy poverty was set free to live and rejoice in the love of his fellow men without obscuring or violating his own personality. Francis's Testament (which is not mentioned in Bonaventura's official life of the saint) shows that he did not waver from his position: "I strictly command all the brethren on obedience that . . . they shall not dare to ask for any letter from the Roman court . . . neither for purposes of preaching nor because of any persecution of their bodies."

There is an episode which illustrates how consistent was Francis's belief in uncloistered Christianity. In 1220 he ordered the abolition of the house of studies at Bologna, founded by Pietro Staccia, Provincial-Minister of the Franciscans and a distinguished lawyer. "You are trying to destroy my order; it is my desire and will that my brethren, following the example of Jesus Christ, shall give more time to prayer than to study." Francis cursed Staccia, it is said, and to his dying day refused to abrogate the curse. Francis knew what he was about. The new theologians were imprisoning God within their philosophical system, bend-

ing divinity to their own wills and objects. The canon lawyers, the
jurists of the Church, were endeavouring to transform the Roman household of the Pope into a stronghold of power. In the
course of this struggle to assert the rights of the Curia and the
Church the medieval Papacy fought its way up to its highest
eminence and to its ruin.

The household was a basic unit in the medieval world—fortified houses, in other words castles, patrician houses in towns,
manor houses, bishops' houses, monastic houses. It is under-
standable that such a society should have tried to bring some
order into the growing horde of "lesser brothers," "friars minor"
as they called themselves from 1216, congregating around St.
Francis. And so an Order was founded. Francis and his earliest
and closest companions had been laymen. By 1219-20 the brotherhood was definitely a Religious Order. Some years before his
death Francis was forced by illness to give up his leadership of
the Order; however, he tried to see to it that the principles of
poverty, itinerant preaching and manual labour were retained
and incorporated into the revised Rule he was asked to compose
about this time, although in other respects he had to compromise. In the Rule which finally received papal approbation (by
Honorius III in 1223) known as the Regula Secunda or Bullata,
the all-important poverty clauses were struck out or modified;
complete poverty was henceforth to be practised only by individuals, and there is no mention of haphazard itinerant preaching. The Franciscans were now an Order, like all the other Orders
prepared to fight for their privileges in every town in Christendom; their chief rivals were the Dominicans, their closest contemporaries. Inevitably, the friars minor became entangled in the
affairs of bishops and parish priests and of men of all kinds; and
they were drawn into the academic atmosphere of the universities.

Francis spent his last years in the crucifying knowledge that his
ideals were being mutilated. Through his perpetual contemplation of the crucified Christ he became deeply identified with

Christ's suffering; shortly before his death he discovered on his own body lesions corresponding to the five wounds of his Lord. He took the utmost care to conceal this terrifying happening from the small group of loyal companions with whom he was now living and whose protection he made his last concern. The dearest of them was probably Leo, the subject of the only two surviving documents written in the saint's own hand. One is a letter: "Brother Leo, your brother Francis sends you his greeting and peace. My son, I am talking to you like a mother, summing up in this letter all the words and advice that passed between us on the way: in whatever way it seems to you that you can be most pleasing to the Lord our God, and best follow in his footsteps and imitate his poverty, do it, with the blessing of the Lord God and in my obedience. And if it is necessary for your soul's sake or your consolation that you should come to me, and if you want to do it, then, Leo, come."

This is utterly free from complaint and recrimination, as indeed were the last years and days of the saint's life, when he was bequeathing to the world his most precious and most personal legacy, adding a new note to the scale of humanity: joy born of perfect and explicit surrender to suffering, willingness to taste the bitterest of this world's fruits. At Assisi, in the garden of the Minoresses of San Damiano, the dying man who had seen his work destroyed could yet sing the Canticle of the Sun. This orginally ended with the praise of God in "our sister, mother earth." But now, when civil war was once again threatening Assisi, Francis sent the contending parties a hymn of peace, which became the penultimate verse of the Canticle:

> Be praised, my Lord, for those who for Thy love forgive
> Contented unavenged in quiet to live.
> Blest those who in the way of peace are found—
> By thee O Lord most high shall they be crowned."

As death drew nearer Francis allowed his brothers to write down his praise of "sister death":

Be praised, my Lord, for our sister bodily death
From whom none can escape that hath drawn breath . . .
Praise ye and bless my Lord and do Him service due
With humblest thanks for all He has done for you.

Very close now to death, he had himself laid on the bare earth, and with his left hand on the wound in his side said "I have done what I had to do; may Christ teach you what is your part." He died soon after sunset on October 3, 1226, at the small hermitage of the Porziuncola near Assisi.

Francis had loosened the tongues and opened the eyes of the Italian people, dispersing the choking fumes of anxiety and hatred which surrounded them. Francis's appeal to the masses is echoed in the Italian vernacular poetry, secular and religious, known as *laude* and in the sublime paintings produced under Franciscan inspiration in the thirteenth and fourteenth centuries. Here at last a valid reconciliation was achieved, the reconciliation of man with himself, with his brother men and with sister earth, an acceptance of the fact that all alike were rooted in the God-given reality of all created things.

Friars minor took a leading part in the "Great Halleluja," a peace-movement which captured many Italian towns in northern Italy: at Parma, Brothers Benedict and Gerardo, at Piacenza Brother Leo. The "Great Halleluja" swept through the whole region like a spring storm, a clap of Whitsuntide thunder. Ancient feuds were healed, warring adversaries became reconciled; everyone was filled with brotherly love and did penance in an access of tears and joy.

Then the spring ran dry. The daily warfare continued. It is evident that the great Franciscan religious poetry (a high-water mark of European achievement in this genre) was the work of men convinced of the reality of endless suffering. The *Dies Irae, Dies Illa,* still the core of the Roman Church's liturgy for the dead, comes from the heart of a Franciscan shocked by his saint into proclaiming the sufferings, fears and hopes of mankind. Suffering and joy are inseparable in this Franciscan hymn, or rather poem —it is both secular and religious. The greatest writer of folk-inspired *laude* may also have been the author of another of the great medieval Latin hymns, the *Stabat Mater*. This was Jacopone da Todi (born 1230, died 1306), a lawyer of noble birth and worldy habits, who became a lay-brother of the Franciscan Order after the death of his wife at a banquet as the result of a horrifying accident. Jacopone delighted to praise the holy poverty of Francis. As a friar minor and open supporter of the Colonna, he was imprisoned for five years by Pope Boniface VIII and only liberated on the Pope's death.

As one looks upwards towards Assisi from the slope of Mount Subasio, covered with olive trees and crossed with the little walls of numerous smallholdings, the eye is met by serried tiers of masonry. On the summit stands the Church of San Francesco, the burial place of St. Francis, fortified by its massive substructure of other buildings thrusting boldly outward from the mountainside. The two churches, the enormous convent with its pillared court-yards, the twelve turrets, together make up one tremendous cita-del. It is true that all this was not built in a day. But it was the building of this vast burial church and the collection of the corre-spondingly vast sums of money needed for it that first brought out into the open in 1230 the conflict between the two opposing parties within the Order, which was to continue for centuries although the name and style of the factions might change. In the first half of the fourteenth century it seemed that the Order would disintegrate into a number of heretical groups. By the fifteenth century this danger had been averted, only to be re-placed by the threat of fresh dissensions between the Observants, who wanted to return to Francis's original ideals, and the Con-ventuals, with the "neutrals" as a third force. The building of the basilica had been a symbol of the victory of the Conventual fac-tion over the "Spiritual," that is over the party which appealed to Francis's Testament and its demand for absolute poverty.

Those who claimed to be St. Francis's spiritual descendants

were to meet with little success. While the saint's closest and dearest companions, a Leo or a Giles, disappeared from the public gaze into the silence of small remote country communities, the zelanti, the Spirituals, became a party of fanatics, who throughout the thirteenth century competed with the Conventuals for the control of the Order. Elias of Cortona, leader of the Conventuals, who presided over the building of the basilica at Assisi and was from 1231 Minister-General of the Order, was relentless in his harrying of the Spirituals; their leader, Caesarius of Speyer, was even imprisoned. By 1239 the burden of Elias's dictatorship had become intolerable to the Order; he was deprived of his office by the Pope and afterwards became a political partisan of the Emperor Frederick II. The first Minister-General to represent the Spirituals was John of Parma (between 1247 and 1257). During his Generalate, however, there appeared the first omens of the catastrophe which was to overtake them. In 1255 a friar from Pisa, Gerard of Borgo San Donnino, was condemned to life imprisonment. Gerard had written an Introduction to a treatise of Abbot Joachim of Flora, and published the two together in Paris. Gerard's Introduction related Joachim's third Dispensation, which was to supplant the carnal Church, to the coming of the Spiritual Franciscans. The Order now came to have a distinctly Joachimite wing, who looked on themselves as the chosen men of the future, the predestined successors of the papal Church. . . . What is relevant here is to notice that their compromising association with ecstatic prophecies made the Spirituals the victims of successive persecutions, which continued to dog them until well into the later fourteenth century.

There grew up around the Spirituals an atmosphere of intellectual and religious unrest and speculation, capable of fostering the scientific studies of a Roger Bacon and the philosophical and political theorizing of a William of Ockham, the late medieval Franciscan whose political sympathies lay with the Empire. Persecuted Spirituals fled from Italy to southern France, Spain and the East. In the last year of the thirteenth century, for example, we hear of some going to Armenia.

These "left-wing" Franciscans, unlike Francis himself, were protesting against the world as they found it; against the growing worldliness within their own Order and its involvement in politics, against domination of the Order by the papal Curia, which turned it into a willing tool in dispensing papal propaganda and in bolstering up the Inquisition.

The defeat of St. Francis within his own Order was not without its therapeutic effects. It meant that in some Franciscan convents there was always a welcome for radical thinking, in religion, philosophy or politics; the prevailing opinion in such houses was compounded of animosity towards Rome and loyal veneration of the memory of the Poor Man of Assisi as the leader of a new age for Christianity and mankind, Christ born again to free his brothers from the chains of the Law.

Saint Francis As Religious Revolutionary

The great movement of ideas in the thirteenth century was a religious movement that had a double character: it was popular and it was lay. It spring from the very heart of the people, and it was ready to grab the sacred from the clergy despite its own uncertainties.

The conservatives of our day who look back at the thirteenth century as the golden age of authoritative religion make an egregious misjudgment. If it was the century *par excellance* of *saints,* it was also the century of *heretics.* We will soon see that the two words are not as contradictory as they appear at first blush; suffice it to say here that never before was the church so strong and so menaced.

There was an attempt at a real religious revolution, and had it succeeded there would have been a universal priesthood and a declaration of the rights of the individual conscience.

The attempt failed, and if much later the revolution made us all kings, neither the thirteenth century nor the Reformation made us all priests. Thus, without a doubt, lies before us the intimate contradiction of our own time which periodically im-

From Paul Sabatier, *Vie de Saint François D'Assise* (Paris: Fischbacher, 1894), pp. v-xvi. Translated from the French by the editor.

perils our national institutions: we are emancipated politically; we are still enslaved both morally and religiously.

This revolution, which has still not ended, was undertaken in the thirteenth century with youthful vigor.

In the north of Europe it took the form of cathedrals, while in the south it was incarnated in its saints.

The cathedrals were the lay churches of the thirteenth century. Constructed by the people and for the people, they were truly the city centers of our ancient towns. Museums, granaries, chambers of commerce, justice halls, archives, and even labor pools—they were all these at one and the same time.

This art of the Middle Ages—which Victor Hugo and Viollet-le-Duc have taught us to understand and love—was the clear expression of the enthusiasm of a people who were becoming conscious of common liberties. Not only were they not the gift of the church, they were a half-conscious protest of the hieratic, immobile, and esoteric art of the monastic orders. From the long list of master builders and artists who created the Gothic monuments of Europe, we learn the names of laymen only. These inspired artists, like those of ancient Greece, could speak to the crowd without vulgarity, for they were, for the most part, common workmen. They found their inspirations not from monastic formularies but from their constant intercourse with the very soul of the people. Therefore, this period should be of interest less to the archaeologist or historian of architecture and more to the historian of the country itself.

While the northern countries were builiding churches and finding in that art something unique, original, and complete, the people of the south were saluting and consecrating a new priesthood beyond that of the official ranks of the clergy. It was the priesthood of the saints.

The priest of the thirteenth century was the very antithesis of the saint—he was almost his enemy. Cut off from the rest of men by his ordination, he inspired awe as the legitimate representative of an all-powerful God; capable of performing unspeakable mysteries by a few symbolic actions, he could, with a word, change bread and wine into flesh and blood. He took on the appearance of an idol who could either be for you or against you and before whom, a person trembled and worshiped.

The saint, on the other hand, had no special vestment to announce his duties; simply through his life and words, he made his mark on the consciences and hearts of all. The saint was without any care of souls in the church, but he felt compelled to raise his voice. The offspring of the common people, he understood all their pains and failings, and their echoing was heard in his own heart. As the prophet of old, he heard a demanding voice speaking to him: "Go and speak to the children of my people.—Lord, I am a child and do not know how to speak.—Say not that 'I am but a child,' for you shall go to those to whom I send you.— Behold I have set you up today as a strong city, a column of iron, and a wall of brass against the kings of Judah and against his leaders and priests."

These saints of the thirteenth century were true prophets. They, like Saint Paul, were apostles not because of a canonical consecration but because they were witnesses of liberty against authority.

When the priest sees himself truly threatened by the prophet, he changes tactics. He takes the prophet under his care. He introduces his sermons into the sacred canon; he throws clerical vestments over his shoulders. Days go by, years roll on, and the common people can no longer distinguish the two. They believe that prophets are spawned by the clergy.

This is one of the most bitter ironies of history.

Francis of Assisi is *par excellance* the saint of the Middle Ages. Deriving nothing either from the church or the school, he was truly a "theodidact"—a God-taught man. And if he only dimly was aware of the revolutionary nature of his preaching, he, at least, always refused ordination to the priesthood. He intuited the superiority of the spiritual priesthood.

What is most attractive about his life is that, thanks to historical records, we can find the man behind the wonder-worker.

We find not merely noble actions. We find a *life* in the deepest sense of that word: I mean we see development and struggle.

How misleading are those hagiographers who put halos and nimbi over his head from the day of his birth! As if the most beautiful spectacle in the world were not that of a man who fights hour after hour to conquer first himself and then all temptations to egotism, idleness, discouragement, finally to find, at the moment when he thinks that he has conquered all, that those who had been attracted to his ideals either ruin his vision completely or render it the most terrible of blows. Poor Francis! The final years of his life were a genuine *via dolorosa* as tortuous as the one suffered by his Master as he sunk under the weight of the cross; it is still a joy to die for one's ideal, but it is a bitter pain indeed to see the total glorification of one's body while one's soul— indeed I would say, one's very thought—is misunderstood and betrayed.

When one seeks out the source of his ideals, they are found exclusively in the people of his own period, and that is why Francis gave flesh and blood to the Italian soul in the thirteenth century just as Dante would do the same a hundred years later.

Francis sprang from the people, and the people recognized themselves in him. He possessed their poetry and their hopes, championed their aspirations; the very name of his group was first and foremost a political commentary: for there was in Assisi, as in most Italian cities, the *Majores* and the *Minores*, the *popolo grasso* and the *popolo minuto*. He identified squarely with the latter. This political side of his mission needs to be clearly appreciated at the offset to fully understand the success of the Franciscans and the originality of its ideology.

As for his attitude vis-à-vis the church, it was one of filial obedience. This may appear a bit odd coming from a preacher without an official mandate who spoke to the world from a sense of personal and immediate inspiration. But did not the greater part of the citizenry in 1789 regard themselves as loyal subjects of Louis XVI?

The church was to our forebears what the state is for us. We may wish to remodel its govermental structure, overturn its constitution, criticize its administration, but we think ourselves patriots in the process.

Much the same way, when there is a simple faith or when the religious sentiment seems to be wedded to the very flesh of humanity, a Dante could attack the clergy and the papal court with a violence that has never been surpassed while still regarding himself a good Catholic. Saint Francis was so certain of the infidelity of the church to her mission that he could speak symbolically of the widowhood of Lady Poverty, who from the time of Christ until his own had found no husband. How could he have better outlined his purpose or revealed his dream?

What he wanted was far more than to found an order, and to restrict his scope to that is to mistake him completely. He fought for a real revival of the church according to an evangelical ideal that he felt that he had rediscovered.

There was a great reawakening when news spread about the penitents who came from that small Umbrian town. It was rumored that they sought a strange favor from the papal court: the right to possess nothing. Men saw them on the road earning their bread by the work of their hands, accepting nothing more than was necessary for their sustenance while giving out to others the bread of life. The people lifted up their heads to breathe in the first drafts of a perfume of entirely fresh flowers.

There are in this world crowds of people capable of heroism if only a leader will guide them. Saint Francis was for them the leader, and the best of humanity at that time were eager to follow his footsteps.

The movement which ended up as a new family of monks was at the beginning antimonastic. To find such contradictions in history is no difficult task. The gentle Galilean who preached a personal revelation without dogmatic law or ceremonial triumphed only to be vanquished, for his words were confiscated by a church that was essentially sacerdotal and dogmatic.

Likewise, the Franciscan movement at the beginning was, if not a protest against monasticism by the Christian conscience, a much more elevated concept of the clergy than had hitherto been known.

Let us picture in our minds the wealthy abbeys of the Benedictines of that epoch. They were veritable fortresses built on summits, where they seem to command the plains below them. Their wealth should come as no surprise. Protected by their very position, they were the only pure shelters for the lovers of peace or the timid of heart. The monks were, in large measure, deserters from the war of life, and often, for motives not always religious, they fled behind the secure walls in those days.

Overlook all this and forget about the demoralized ignorance of the parish clergy, the simony and vice of the prelates, the vulgarity and greed of the monks and judge the church in the thirteenth century only by the very best of its sons—the ones who do the church the most honor. These are the hermits and monks who fled into the desert away from the wars and vices, pausing only long enough to be sure that no outside noise had penetrated the quiet of their contemplative solitude. At times they drew away along with hundreds of their disciples to the solitudes of Clairvaux, Chartreuse, Vallombrosa, and Camaldoli. But even as a multitude, they are alone. They were dead to the world and to their brothers. Each cell was a desert and over it was written:

> *O beata solitudo*
> *O sola beatitudo*
> (Blessed solitude/sole beatitude)

The book of the *Imitation* is the picture of this life of the cloister that is best and purest.

But this denial of action—is it really Christian?

Saint Francis thought not. As far as he was concerned, he wanted to act like Christ, and his imitation of Christ was more closely aligned to Christ than that of Thomas a Kempis.

Jesus went out into the desert but only to find in prayer and communion with the Father the strength and force necessary to continue the combat against the forces of evil. He did not avoid the multitude; he sought them out to console, enlighten, and convert them.

This is what Saint Francis wanted to imitate. More than once he felt the seductive charm of the purely contemplative life, but each time his own intuition was that such was disguised egotism. To save himself he must save others.

When he saw pain and the misery of corruption, he had no mind to flee; he stopped to heal and bind up with a heart brimming with compassion. He did not simply preach love to others; he was enthralled by it; he sang of it; what is best: he lived it.

There had been preachers of love before his time, but, for the most part, they made an appeal to a certain vulgar selfishness. They believed that one triumphed, for in giving they put their love out for usurious interest. Saint Peter Chrysologus wrote, "Give to the poor, for you are giving to yourself. Give him a crumb, and get back a loaf. Give him a home to receive heaven."

There is nothing of this in Saint Francis, whose charity extended beyond; it was pure love. He went not to the healthy, who had no need of a doctor; he went to the sick, the forgotten, the dregs. He lavished the treasures of his heart according to need and saved the best for those who were the most poor and the most despised: thieves and lepers.

He gained immeasurably through the lacks in his formal education. Better educated, the formal logic of the schools could have robbed him of the simplicity of his manner, which is one of the great charms of his life. He would have understood the full nature of the church's illness and despaired of healing it. If he had been conversant with the full range of ecclesiastical discipline, he would have felt constrained to observe it; being ignorant of it, he could be a heretic unawares.

We can now better determine what religious strain Saint Francis belongs to.

Looking at the question from a detached viewpoint, one sees that, in the last analysis, souls like religious systems fall into one of two great strains that are two poles of thought. These are not mathematical polarities, for in the concrete they rarely exist, but we can set them down on the map of philosophical or moral ideas.

There are religions that orient themselves toward the Divine, while others look to mankind. Again let it be repeated that this is a line of demarcation between two strains that is purely idealistic and contrived; they so very often intermingle that it is difficult to distinguish them especially in the area of our own culture. However, when we go back to the sources, the characteristics of each becomes much more clear.

Among the religions that are oriented towards the Divine, the primary emphasis is on cult and, especially, sacrifice. The goal of these religions is a change in the attitude of the gods. The gods are all-powerful kings whose favor is bought or guaranteed by gifts.

The greater part of the pagan religions belong to this category, as does pharisaic Judaism. There is also a tendency in certain conservative Catholic quarters to appease God or "buy off" the Virgin by candles and masses.

The other religions are more oriented toward man. Their efforts are directed toward the heart and the conscience in an attempt to change them. Sacrifice either disappears or is interiorized. God is seen as a father who welcomes all who approach him. Conversion, perfection, and sanctification become the preeminent religious acts. Cult and prayer become less an incantation; they take on the aspect of meditation, reflection, and struggle. Religions of the first type see priests as essential intermediaries between heaven and earth, while those of this type deemphasize the priesthood and enter into direct relationship with God.

It was given to the prophets of Israel to delineate precisely this religion of the Spirit:

Bring no more vain offerings;
I loathe your incense,
your new moons, your Sabbaths, and your assemblies;
When you multiply prayers, I will not listen.
Your hands are bloodstained;
wash and make yourself clean.
Take away from my eyes the evil of your ways,
cease to do evil,
learn to do good.

These considerations are useful in trying to reach out to the spiritual ancestors of Saint Francis of Assisi.

For Saint Francis, as for Paul and Augustine, conversion meant a complete and radical personal change—the act by which the will throws off the servitude of sin in order to take on the yoke of divine authority. Prayer becomes an essential act of life while losing completely its magical character. It is the élan of the heart; it is the reflection and meditation that transcends the vulgarities of this life to help one penetrate and conform to the Divine Will. It is the act of the atom which appreciates its littleness but which desires, even though it is a minor note, to be in harmony with the divine symphony.

Ecce adsum, Domine, ut faciam voluntatem tuam
(Here I am, Lord, to do thy will)

When one reaches these heights, he no longer belongs to a sectarian movement; he belongs to humanity. He is like those miracles of nature that chance had given to this or that land but which in reality belongs to all people, for they are the common and inalienable property of all. Homer, Shakespeare, Dante, Goethe, Rembrandt, and Michelangelo belong to all of us, as do the ruins of Greece and Rome. Or better, they belong to all those who love or understand them the best.

But that which is a truism when one speaks of men of reason or geniuses of the imagination becomes a paradox when one speaks of religious genius. The church has laid such a claim on them that it appears that she owns them by some sort of right. It cannot be that this act of confiscation will endure forever. To stop it an act of demolition or negation is hardly necessary. Let them have their chapels and relics, and, far from denigrating the saints, let us exalt them in all their true grandeur.

Saint Francis in the Legends

These Are the Little Flowers of Saint Francis and His Brothers

First of all, one should consider that the glorious Saint Francis, in all the deeds of his life, patterned himself after Christ. Just as Christ chose twelve disciples at the beginning of his preaching and taught them to despise the world, to follow him in poverty, and to be schooled in every virtue, so also Saint Francis chose twelve followers at the foundation of his order to follow poverty in the most exalted manner.

Just as one of the Apostles of Christ, abandoned by God, hung himself, so also one of the twelve followers of Saint Francis, Giovanni della Capella by name, left the order and in the end also hung himself. For all the elect of God this was an example and a spur to humility and fear of the Lord, since no one can expect to persevere to the end except through the grace of God.

Just as the Holy Apostles were known throughout the whole world as marvels of sanctity, filled with the Holy Spirit, so also the holy companions of Saint Francis were men of such sanctity

---

Selected and translated by the editor from the *Fioretti*.

that the world had not known such holy and spirit-filled men since the days of the Apostles. One, Brother Egidio, was swept into the third heaven like Saint Paul; another, Brother Filippo Lungo, was touched on the lips by a flaming coal through the intervention of an angel, just as it had happened in the case of the prophet Isaiah. Another brother, Silvestro by name, spoke to God face to face just like Moses. Brother Bernardo, much like the evangelist Saint John, flew to the light of Divine Wisdom like an eagle by means of the clarity of his intellect. This same Brother Bernard, the most humble of men, was a most profound commentator on the Holy Scriptures. Brother Ruffino, a nobleman of Assisi, was sanctified by God and canonized in heaven, while he was still on this earth.

All were thus blessed with singular signs of sanctity, as this narrative will show.

[Chapter I]

How Saint Francis Converted Signor Bernardo of Assisi

Brother Bernardo of Assisi was the first companion of Saint Francis. He was converted in the following manner.

Although he had already turned his back on the world and as a penance allowed himself to be scorned and abused, Saint Francis still wore secular clothes. Many of the people thought he had gone crazy, and they derided him as a madman, so that relatives and strangers alike threw stones and mud at him. But Francis bore every abuse with the patience of a deaf-mute. Signor Bernardo of Assisi (who was one of the richest, wisest, and noblest men of the city) was struck by the contempt that Saint Francis had for the world, his great patience in the face of scorn, and the fact that he bore up under two years of misuse and personal humiliation. He seemed so patient and cheerful that Bernardo mused to himself, "This Francis must be highly favored by God."

One evening Bernardo invited Francis to eat and spend the night with him, and Francis accepted the invitation. Signor Bernardo was determined to observe his holiness, so he fixed a bed for him in the same room with himself and kept a light burning in the room. Saint Francis, to hide his sancity, went right to his bed when he entered the room and began to feign asleep. Bernardo, after a short wait, did likewise and after a bit, with loud snoring, was sound asleep. When Saint Francis was convinced that Signor Bernardo was really and truly asleep, he got up and began to pray. Joining his hands together and raising his eyes to heaven, Francis spoke with profound devotion and fervor; "My God! My God!" With tears Francis continued this same prayer right until morning, always repeating, "My God! My God!", and nothing else. Saint Francis said this while contemplating and praising the excellence of the Divine Majesty that stooped to a world that was lost to grant to Francis, the little poor man, and to the others of this world the chance for the salvation of their souls. Illumined by the grace of prophecy, he also foresaw the great things that God would work through his order. Dwelling on his own insufficiency and mediocre virtue, he called on God to supply, aid, and fill up through divine pity and omipotence those things that were lacking because of human fragility.

Signor Bernardo saw Saint Francis at his devotions by the light of the candle and, deeply touched by the words of Francis's prayer, was inspired by the Holy Spirit to change the mode of his own life. In the morning he called Saint Francis and said to him, "Brother Francis, I am totally disposed to renounce the world and follow you in total obedience." Hearing this Francis was delighted and answered, "Signor Bernardo, what you have said to me is such a great and glorious thing that we must seek counsel from our Lord Jesus Christ by praying that we may understand what his will is in this matter and how we best may follow it. Let us go to the cathedral where a good priest will say mass for us, and we will remain in prayer until after Tierce. Then we will open the missal three times and see what kind of life God has elected for us." Signor Bernardo was in complete accord with this plan.

They went off to the cathedral and heard mass and then remained in prayer until after Tierce was completed. At the request of Saint Francis, the priest then took the missal, made the sign of the cross over it, and opened it three times in the name of our Lord Jesus Christ. The first time the book was opened to that passage where Jesus spoke to the young man who sought perfection these words: "If you will be perfect, go and sell what you possess, give to the poor, and come follow me." The second reading was the words of Jesus to the Apostles when he was about to send them off to preach: "Take nothing for your journey: neither staff nor bag nor shoes nor money." For he wished by this advice to encourage them to put all their trust in God and to have only one intention: to preach the Gospel. In the third reading there were words of Christ: "He who wishes to come after me should deny himself, take up his cross, and come follow me."

Saint Francis then said to Signor Bernardo, "This is the advice that Christ has given us; go and do exactly as he has advised us. Blessed be our Lord Jesus Christ, who has deigned to show us the path of the Gospel."

Hearing all this Signor Bernardo went out immediately and began to sell all that he had. He was a very rich man, but, with complete joy, he gave all to the poor, widows, orphans, pilgrims, monasteries, and hospitals. In all this Saint Francis gave him both help and encouragement.

A man by the name of Signor Silvestro saw Saint Francis make donations and encourage others to do the same. Overcome by his greed, he said to the saint, "You have not paid me in full for the stones that you got from me to rebuild churches. Now that you have money, I want payment." Saint Francis, stupified by his greed but not wishing to argue with him (as a true believer in the Gospel), took handfuls of money from the lap of Signor Bernardo and dropped them into the lap of Signor Silvestro, telling him at the same time that if he wanted more he should return.

Contented with himself, Signor Silvestro returned home. Later in the evening, he was thinking back and began to chide himself for his greed, comparing it to the sanctity of Signor Bernardo and the holiness of Saint Francis. That evening and on two other nights, he had a vision from God: a cross of gold came out of the mouth of Saint Francis, and the top of it touched the heavens, and the arms extended worldwide from east to west. Because of this vision, he dedicated all to God and became a friar minor. In the order he was so touched by holiness and grace that he spoke with God as a friend speaks to a friend. Saint Francis experienced this more than once, as will be narrated later.

Signor Bernardo, likewise, was so filled with the grace of God that he was often rapt in his contemplation. Saint Francis said of him that he was worthy of every respect, for he was a founder of the order. After all, he was the first to abandon the world, not holding anything back but giving all to the poor of Christ and adopting a life of evangelical poverty, offering himself naked to the embrace of the Crucified One. May he be revered by us for ever and ever.

Amen.

[Chapter II]

How Saint Francis and Brother Leo Said Morning Prayer Without a Breviary

Once, in the early days of the order, Saint Francis and Brother Leo found themselves in a place without the books necessary to recite the Divine Office. When the time came for morning prayer, Saint Francis said to Brother Leo, "My dearest friend, we are without a breviary for morning prayer, but we must spend the time in the praise of God, so I will speak and you will answer with the words that I teach you. But be sure and answer exactly as I speak without changing a word. I will say 'Brother Francis, you do so much evil and commit so many sins that you are worthy only of hell,' and you will answer, 'Truly you deserve the deepest part of hell.' " And Brother Leo, with the simplicity of a dove, said, "Agreed, my father, In the name of God, let us begin."

So Saint Francis began: "Brother Francis, you have so many vices and have committed so many sins on this earth that you are worthy of hell." And Brother Leo answered, "God will do good through you, and you will be received into paradise." Saint Francis said, "Don't speak so but answer what I have said: 'Brother Francis, you have done so much evil that you are worthy to be damned by God,' and then say, 'Truly you are worthy to be among the damned.' " And Brother Leo answered, "Just as you wish, father."

Then Saint Francis, with tears and sighs and beating of breast, cried out in a loud voice, "My Lord God of heaven and earth, I have committed so many offenses against you that I am worthy of damnation." And Brother Leo answered, "Brother Francis, among the blessed of God you will be singularly blessed." Saint Francis, marveling that Leo spoke the opposite of what he had been instructed, rebuked him saying, "Why don't you answer as I have ordered? When I say, 'Wretched little Brother Francis, do you think that God will have mercy on you, when you have committed so many sins, even if you are the God of mercy and consolation? You are not worthy of mercy,' I order you under holy obedience to answer what I teach. You are to say, my little lamb of a brother, 'By no means are you worthy to find mercy.' "

But when Saint Francis said, "Wretched little Brother Francis, etc.," Brother Leo answered, "God the Father, whose mercy is infinite and far beyond all sin, will grant you great mercy and grant you many graces."

To this answer Saint Francis, a bit disturbed and wondering at Brother Leo, said to him, "How do you presume to act against holy obedience and insist on answering contrary to the way I have taught you?" Leo answered with great piety and humility, "God be my witness, my father, that every time I'm ready in my heart to answer in the way that you have ordered, God makes me speak as it pleases him rather than as it pleases me."

Saint Francis marveled at this and said to Brother Leo, "I beg you, my beloved friend, to answer this time in the way that I indicate." Brother Leo answered, "Proceed and, in the name of God, I will try to do your will." Saint Francis weepingly said, "Brother Francis, you wretched nothing, etc." And Brother Leo responded, "You will receive great grace from God and be exalted and glorified in heaven, for the humble shall be exalted, And I cannot say otherwise because God speaks through my lips."

And so it went in a humble contest that day with many tears and great spiritual comfort, as they passed the night waiting for the dawn light.

In the praise of Christ. Amen.

[Chapter IX]

How Brother Masseo Tempted Saint Francis

Once Saint Francis was staying at Saint Mary of the Angels along with Brother Masseo, who was a man of great sanctity, discretion, and the grace to speak intimately with God. It was for all these reasons that Saint Francis loved him very much. One day Saint Francis was coming out from the woods where he had been praying. Brother Masseo wished to test his humility, so he came up to him and began to speak to him in a manner that was nearly insulting: "Why you? Why you? Why you?" Saint Francis answered, "What do you mean?" To which Brother Masseo gave this response: "I ask this because men come from all over the world to speak to you or even to get a glance at least; they desire to listen, learn, and then obey you. Why? You are not good looking, not an intellectual, not of the nobility. Why does all the world chase you then?"

Hearing all this, Saint Francis was overjoyed. He raised his face toward the heavens for a long while and then knelt and rendered thanks and praise to God. Only then, in a great spirit, did he turn to Brother Masseo and answer, "Why me? You want to know, Why me? Me? Why they follow me? I have seen the answer in the eyes of the Most High God who sees both evil and good. Those most holy eyes have never seen a sinner so vile, so worthless, and so sinful as myself. To do the marvelous thing that he intends, he could not have found a more unworthy instrument. So he chose me to confound the wise and the beautiful of this world along with its strength and power. In this way everyone can clearly understand that every good thing comes from him and that no man can claim glory in his sight. Anyone who wishes to glory must glory in the Lord, to whom be all praise and honor forever."

Hearing this answer that was so humble and so fervent, Brother Masseo was overcome. He knew with absolute certainty that Saint Francis was firmly anchored in complete humility.

In the praise of Christ. Amen.

[Chapter X]

Saint Francis Holds a General Chapter At Assisi

The faithful servant of Christ, Saint Francis, once held a general meeting at Saint Mary of the Angels to which about five thousand brothers came. Saint Dominic, founder of the Friars Preachers, also came, as he was on his way from Bologna to Rome. He had heard that there was a meeting of the chapter in the fields around Saint Mary of the Angels, so he stopped by with seven of his brothers.

At this meeting there was also a cardinal who was most devoted to Saint Francis. Saint Francis had prophesied that this cardinal would be pope one day, and so it happened. He had come from

Perugia, where the papal court was. He had come to see Saint
Francis and his brothers. On some days he sang mass for them,
and on other days he preached to the brothers. He felt great
delight and edification when he came to visit this gathering. In
the area around Saint Mary of the Angels he would see seated
groups of brothers—here forty, there a hundred, in another place
two or three hundred—all of them occupied solely in thinking
about God, praying, weeping, doing acts of charity, in silence and
modesty without the slightest noise or confusion. He marveled at
such an orderly multitude that acted with tears and great devotion. He said to himself, "Truly this is the camp of the army of
the knights of God." In that whole crowd there were heard no
jokes or idle chatter but only groups of brothers who prayed or
recited the Office or wept for their sins or the sins of their bene-
factors or discussed the salvation of souls.

In the surrounding field, there were huts with roofs made of
rushes or mats, and these huts were divided into the provinces
from which the brothers came. That is why this meeting has often
been called the chapter of the mats or the rushes. Their bed was
the bare earth and, for those who had it, a bit of straw with pillows
of wood or stone. Everyone who heard or saw these things was
moved to great devotion. Such was their fame that from the papal
court, which was in Perugia, and from the valley of Spoleto, there
came counts, barons, knights, other gentlemen, common people,
cardinals, bishops, abbots, clerics, and others just to see the holy
and humble congregation, for the world had never seen such a
meeting of so many holy men in one place. But above all, they
came to see the head and most holy father of this group, who had
stolen such beautiful prey from the world and formed such a
lovely and devoted flock in order to follow in the footsteps of the
great Shepherd, Jesus Christ.

After the whole group had gathered together, the holy father
and minister general of all, Saint Francis, in the fervor of the
Spirit spoke the Word of God and preached in a loud voice to

them with words that God himself suggested. In his sermon, he followed this theme:

My children! We have promised great things to God, but God has promised even greater things to us. Let us observe those things which we have promised and wait in certainity for those things that he has promised to us. The joy of this world is short, but the pain that follows it is of perpetual duration. The pain of this life is nothing compared to the joy of the next.

Using words similar to these, he comforted the brothers and encouraged them to obey and revere Holy Mother the Church; to have fraternal love and to pray for all the people of God; to have patience in adversity and to have temperance in prosperity; to keep away from any impurity and to exalt angelic purity; to cultivate peace and concord with God, man, one's conscience; finally, to love and fully observe holy poverty.

Then he said to them, "By holy obedience, I order that none of you take any care about what you shall eat or drink while at this meeting; just pray and praise God." Then he added, "All cares about your bodily needs should be left in the hands of God, for he has a special care over you." Everyone there received these words with a light heart and a happy countenance. And when Saint Francis finished preaching, all the assembled brothers returned to their prayers.

Saint Dominic, who was present at the sermon, was somewhat perplexed at the orders of Saint Francis. He thought it indiscreet that provision had not been made for material necessities, considering the vast size of the group assembled there.

But the chief pastor, the Blessed Christ, wishing to demonstrate the care that he has for his flock and his poor, inspired the people of Perugia, Spoleto, Foligo, Spello, and Assisi, along with others in the vicinity, to bring foodstuffs and drink to the chapter meeting. Soon men came from these areas with pack animals, horses, and carts full of bread, wine, beans, cheese, and other such good things to eat as the poor of Christ are wont to need.

They also brought clothes, glasses, pitchers, and other utensils that the crowd needed. Those that could bring more or help more considered it a blessing. Even the knights, barons, and other nobility that had come to observe helped to serve with great humility and devotion.

When Saint Dominic saw all this, he realized that Divine Providence watched over the group and that his judgment about the indiscretion of Saint Francis had been false. Humbly he knelt before him, spoke of his error, and added, "God truly has a special solicitude for these little poor men, and I did not know it. From now on I vow to observe evangelical poverty, and I curse, in the name of God, any brother in my order who presumes to hold property." Saint Dominic was greatly edified by the faith of Saint Francis and by the obedience and proverty of those present at the chapter and by the providence of God and by the great quantity of things that they received by relying on this providence.

At this same meeting Saint Francis learned that many of the brothers were wearing penitential vests of iron and iron bands under their habits. This had caused grave illness for many and death for some and had proved to be a general hindrance to prayer. Saint Francis, as a prudent father, ordered that all such vests of iron and bands be brought to him and laid at his feet. This was done, and there numbered over five hundred vests of iron and even more bands that had been worn on legs or around the stomachs, so the whole collection made a large pile. Saint Francis left them all there. When the meeting broke up, Saint Francis comforted them all in the good and taught them how to avoid the evils of this world. Then he sent them back to their provinces filled with holy joy.

To the praise of Christ. Amen.

[Chapter XVIII]

How Saint Francis Went To Convert the Sultan of Egypt

Saint Francis, fired by his zeal for Christ and a desire for martyrdom, once took twelve holy companions and journeyed across the ocean to go directly to the sultan of Egypt. When he arrived at the territory of the Saracens, the passes were guarded by ferociously cruel men who allowed no Christian to pass alive. However, it pleased God to save them all from death, but they were beaten, bound, and taken in chains to the sultan.

Before the sultan Saint Francis, filled with the Holy Spirit, preached the faith of Christ so fervently that he was even prepared to be tested by fire. The sultan was quite touched by this devotion, by his steadfast faith, and by the utter worldlessness that he saw in him. Saint Francis would not accept any gift, even though he was the poorest of men. He was concerned only to suffer willingly for his faith. The sultan, as a result of this, listened to him willingly, granted both he and his companions permission to preach where they wished, and invited him to come often to see him. He also gave them a safe-conduct so that they would not be harmed by his followers

Armed with this permission, Saint Francis sent his companions two by two to different parts of the country to preach the faith of Christ. He chose one area and with a brother went there. On arrival, they stopped at an inn to rest. At the inn there was a woman, beautiful in body but tainted in soul, who tempted Saint Francis to sin. Saint Francis said, "I accept your proposition. Let us be off to bed." She led him to a room, and Saint Francis said to her, "I will show you a beautiful bed." There was a great fire there in the fireplace, and Saint Francis, rapt by the Spirit, stripped off his clothes and entered the fire and then invited the girl to likewise undress and come join him in that beautiful spot.

Saint Francis stood in that fire for a long time with a smiling face and was neither burned nor even scorched. The girl was so overcome by this miracle and so penitent in her heart for her sin that she not only repented her evil but converted perfectly to the Faith of Christ, and through her many other souls were saved in that area.

After a bit Saint Francis realized that he could do no more in those parts and, through the intervention of divine guidance, decided to send all of his companions back to the Christian lands. All together they went back to the sultan to make their good-byes. The sultan said to him, "Francis, I would most happily embrace the Faith of Christ, but I fear to do so now. For if those about me heard of it, they would kill not only me but you and all your companions. Since there is so much good that you can do and there are so many grave duties that I must discharge, I am unwilling to provoke either your death or mine. So tell me what I must do to be saved, and I will follow your advice as best I can."

Saint Francis responded, "My Lord, I must go now and return to my country. After my return, when by the grace of God my death has come, and I have gone to heaven, I will send you two friars who will come to you to baptize you in the name of Christ, and so you will be saved. My Lord Jesus Christ has revealed this to me. In the interim, free yourself from all entanglements so that when the grace of God comes, he may find you devout and faithful." This the sultan promised, and this he did.

After this Saint Francis and his companions returned to their land, and after a time Francis died and rendered his soul to God. The sultan, informed of the death, set guards at all the frontiers with instructions that if two men should come with clothing similar to that of Saint Francis, they should be brought to the sultan without the least delay to bring him the promised salvation. In the meantime Saint Francis appeared to two friars and told them to go across the ocean to the sultan and bring him the long-sought-after salvation. They immediately complied, and the guards on seeing them brought them to the sultan. The sultan received them with great joy and said, "Now I know that the good God has sent his servants for my salvation, just as Saint Francis promised me after his divine revelation." Receiving the instruction of the Faith of Christ, he was baptized by the brothers and regenerated in Christ. He later died of his illness, and his soul was saved by the merits and intervention of Saint Francis.

In the praise of Christ. Amen.

[Chapter XXIV]

How Saint Francis Healed a Leper in Body and Soul

The true disciple of Christ, Saint Francis, while he was living in this miserable life, tried to follow in the path of Christ with all his strength, for Christ was the perfect master. So it often happened that as he healed a body, God also healed the soul, for the same thing often happened to Christ. So Francis not only served lepers willingly but also ordered his brethren as they went about the world to serve the needs of lepers for the love of Christ, who was reputed a poor leper himself.

It happened once that Saint Francis was staying in a place near to where some of the brothers of the order were serving a leper hospital. There was a leper there who was testy, unruly, and so obstinate that everyone believed—and they were not wrong— that he was possessed. He abused and cursed whoever waited on him and, what was worse, bitterly blasphemed and cursed Christ and his Holy Mother. No one wanted to take care of him or be near him.

The brothers were quite willing to put up with his many abuses in order to grow in the virtue of patience, but their consciences would not tolerate his blasphemies about Christ and his Mother.

They were quite prepared to abandon him, but they thought that before doing this they should consult Saint Francis, who was staying nearby.

Hearing what they had to say, Saint Francis went to see the perverse leper. Finding him, Francis greeted him warmly: "God grant you peace, my dearest brother."

The leper replied with a grumble, "What peace can I find from God, who has taken away my peace and every worldly good and left me cancerous and stinking?"

Saint Francis answered, "My son, be patient! God often inflicts us with a weakness of the body for the good of our souls. There is great merit in bearing illness with patience."

But the sick man retorted, "How can I endure the continual pain both day and night with any sense of peace? Not only am I sick, but the brothers who were sent to help me will not do it, as they ought."

Saint Francis, divinely inspired to understand that this leper was possessed by an evil spirit, prayed most devoutly for this man before God. After he had prayed, he returned again to speak to the leper: "My son, I will take care of you, since the others do not want to."

"I'll willingly have you. What can you do though that the others have not done?"

"What do you want me to do?"

"I want you to wash me, for I stink so bad that I cannot stand myself."

Saint Francis immediately went and heated water, which he scented with herbs. Then he undressed the man and washed him with his own hands, while another brother poured the water. Through divine power, wherever Saint Francis touched him with his hands, the leprosy disappeared and the flesh grew immediately healthy. And as his body healed, so also did his soul. When the leper saw his body heal, he began to weep bitterly because of his sorrow for his sins and the great compunction that he felt. As his body was cleansed from the leprosy by the bathing, so his soul was cleansed by the cleansing power of his tears and his sorrow. When he was perfectly healed in both soul and body, he humbly felt his weakness and cried out with a loud voice, "Woe is me! I am fit only for hell because of the evil things that I said to the brothers and for the blasphemies and insults that I uttered against God." He continued in a bitter fit of tears about his sins and asked for mercy from God and confessed all his faults to the priest.

Saint Francis, aware of the clear miracle that God had performed through his hands, fled to a distant country, for he feared lest he be the recipient of any worldly fame because of the miracle. He preferred that God alone be honored by the work and wanted no honor for himself.

Through the working of God's will, the leper, now healed in body and soul, died of another sickness within fifteen days of his cure, and strengthened by the sacraments, his soul went right to paradise.

Soon afterward he appeared to Saint Francis, who was in a wooded spot praying. "Do you recognize me?" he said. "Who are you?" Saint Francis replied. And the leper answered him, "I am the leper which the blessed Christ healed through your merits. Today I have been received in paradise, and I render thanks to him and to you. May your soul and body be blessed, and blessed be your words and works, for through you many souls will be saved. You should also understand that not one day passes without the angels and saints thanking God for the fruits that you and your order harvest in the world. Therefore be thankful and comforted in the blessing of God." And finishing these words, he went into paradise. Saint Francis was greatly consoled.

In the praise of Christ. Amen.

[Chapter XXV]

How Saint Francis and Brother Ruffino Preached Naked in the Streets of Assisi

Brother Ruffino contemplated and prayed so much that he was very withdrawn, rarely spoke, and became almost a recluse. Nor did he have much ability in preaching or the use of words. Nonetheless, one day Saint Francis told him to go to Assisi and preach to the people, using the words that God would inspire him to use.

Brother Ruffino, on hearing the order, said to Saint Francis, "Reverend father, I beg you not to send me, for, as you know, I have no talent for preaching, being an unlettered, simple, and not too bright soul." Saint Francis answered, "Because you did not obey with alacrity, I order you to strip down to your breeches, walk through the city of Assisi, find a church there, and preach to the people."

At this order Brother Ruffino stripped himself and naked made his way to Assisi. Entering a church, he genuflected before the altar, climbed up into pulpit, and began to speak. Children and men alike began to laugh and cry out, "Look at him! They have done so much penance, they have gone crazy."

Saint Francis, in the meantime, began to think about the obedience of Brother Ruffino, a man who was one of the most noble of Assisi. It was a harsh order to give, and he began to reprove himself: "What presumption you have, son of Pietro Bernardone, you wretched little creature. How dare you send Brother Ruffino, one of the noblest men of Assisi, to walk through the streets naked like some madman. By God, you will do the same thing that you have ordered the other to do."

With that, he stripped naked and departed right off for Assisi, taking with him Brother Leo (who was clothed), who carried his habit and that of Brother Ruffino. As he came near the town, the citizens began to taunt him, thinking that he had gone crazy from his excessive penances.

Saint Francis went into the church where Brother Ruffino was preaching in these words: "My beloved people, flee the world; avoid sin; help each other if you wish to avoid hellfire; observe the commandments of God; love God and your neighbor if you wish to go to heaven; do penance if you wish to possess the heavenly kingdom." Saint Francis, completely nude, then ascended the pulpit and began to preach so powerfully about despising the world, penance, voluntary poverty, the desire for the kingdom of God, nudity, and poverty of the crucified Christ that the people, on hearing it, all began to cry with copious tears. A vast number of men and women felt great devotion and compunction of heart.

Soon what happened in the church overflowed into the whole city, so that the passion of Christ had never been mourned more than on that day. The people were edified and consoled by Saint Francis and Brother Ruffino. Saint Francis dressed Brother Ruffino, and the two of them headed back to Saint Mary of the Angels, praising and glorifying God, who had given them the grace to forget and humiliate themselves for the edification of the flock of Christ, who learned about despising the world. The acquired such a reputation of holiness from this incident that the people thought it was a grace just to touch the hem of their habit.

In the praise of Christ. Amen.

[Chapter XXX]

Saint Francis on Himself

To me, Brother Francis, the Lord thus gave the grace to do penance: when I was still a sinner, I thought it too bitter a thing to look at lepers, and the Lord led me to them and taught me to be merciful; after leaving them, that which seemed bitter now appeared as sweetness both for soul and body. I tarried a bit and then left the world. In the churches the Lord gave me such faith that I was able to pray simply and say, "We adore you, Lord Jesus Christ, here and in all the churches of the whole world, and we bless you because by your holy cross you have redeemed the world."

The Lord then gave me, and grants me today, a great faith in the priests who live according to the usage of the church because of their holy orders, and even if they persecuted me, I would have recourse to them. And even if I were to possess the wisdom of Solomon and were to come up on the poor priests of this world, I would not preach in their churches if they were unwilling to have me. I would continue to love, honor, and respect them as well as other priests. They are my superiors. I wish to see no sin in them, for in them I see the Son of God, and they are my lords. And I act thus because I see nothing with the eyes of the body

---

The last testament of Francis of Assisi. Translated from the Latin by the editor.

in this world of the most high Son of God except the body and blood which they receive and administer to others. I wish that these exalted mysteries be honored, venerated, and maintained in precious places. Anytime that I have found the holy names or the sacred writings in indecorous places, I have wished to gather them in decent places, and I wish that others will also do the same. Thus we should honor and venerate all theologians and others who dispense the Word of God as those who give spirit and life.

When the Lord had entrusted brothers to me, nobody told me how to treat them; but the Most High revealed to me personally that I ought to live according to the norm of the Holy Gospel. I had it all written in a few simple words, and the lord pope approved it. And those who wished to embrace this life gave the poor everything they had and contented themselves with a tunic patched inside and out and a belt and some underclothes. And we did not wish anything more.

We clerics recited the Office just as other clerics do and the lay members recited the Lord's Prayer; we remained with alacrity in the churches. We were simple and subject to all. And I did manual labor and wished to do it; I hope that all the brothers will do honest work with their hands. Those who are not skilled in work should learn not in order to gain a good wage for their effort but in order to give a good example and avoid idleness. When the reward of work is not forthcoming, we return to the table of the Lord in begging door to door.

The Lord has revealed to me that we ought to give the following greeting to others: "May the Lord give you peace." Let the brothers beware of accepting churches, poor inhabitations, or other constructions made for them unless they conform to the demands of holy poverty, as we have promised in the rule to live always as wayfarers and pilgrims.

I make it an imperative demand of obedience that no brother dare accept any privilege from the Roman Curia, either by himself on through an intermediary, for a church or any other place using the pretext of the needs of preaching or a refuge from persecution; rather, if they are not received, let them flee to another area and there do penance with the blessing of God. I wish firmly to obey the minister general of this brotherhood and whatever guardian it pleases him to appoint over me. I want to be a slave in his hands, not moving or acting in the least manner without his wish, for he is my master. And even though I am weak and simple, I want a cleric with me always to recite the Office with me, as it is established in the rule.

In a similar manner all the other brothers are obliged by obedience to obey their guardians and to recite the Office according to the rule. And if anyone is found who does not say the Office according to the rule, or who varies it or who is not Catholic, let all the brothers, wherever they may be, be held in obedience to turn that brother over to the guardian of the place that is nearest to them. And that minister is to watch him night and day as a prisoner in bonds until the moment when he can turn the brother over to his own minister. And the minister is bound by obedience to watch him night and day like a prisoner in bonds and have him escorted by brothers to the lord of Ostia who is the master, protector, and corrector of the whole brotherhood.

No brother should say, "This is another rule"; for this is a testament, a memorial, an exhortation, and a remembrance that I, the little Brother Francis, have made for you, my blessed brothers, so that you will better be able to observe the holy rule that we have promised before the Lord. The minister general and all the other ministers and guardians are obliged by obedience to neither add nor subtract from these words. In fact, they should carry a copy of this along with the rule, and in all the meetings when they read the rule, this also should be read. All my brothers, clerical and lay, are ordered in obedience to make glosses neither on the rule nor on these words; neither should they say, "They should be interpreted thusly"; rather, as the Lord told me what to say and how to write this rule purely and simply, they are to observe this rule and these words simply and purely and fulfill them right to the end.

Whoever has observed these things will be filled with the heavenly benediction of the Most High Father and on earth be filled with the blessing of his beloved Son and the Most Holy Spirit, the Paraclete, and all the heavenly powers and the saints. And I, Brother Francis, your little one and your servant, inasmuch as I can, will strengthen you within and without with this most holy blessing.

Amen.

FRANCIS AND NATURE

"Oak." 1964. Pencil on paper. 28½" x 22½". Artist: Ellsworth Kelly. Courtesy of Ellsworth Kelly. From a private collection in New York City. Photograph by Geoffrey Clements.

PART TWO

Francis of Assisi and Nature

St. Francis and Nature

St. Francis was not a lover of nature. Properly understood, a lover of nature was precisely what he was not. The phrase implies accepting the material universe as a vague environment, a sort of sentimental pantheism. In the romantic period of literature, in the age of Byron and Scott, it was easy enough to imagine that a hermit in the ruins of a chapel (preferably by moonlight) might find peace and a mild pleasure in the harmony of solemn forests and silent stars, while he pondered over some scroll or illuminated volume, about the liturgical nature of which the author was a little vague. In short, the hermit might love nature as a background. Now for St. Francis nothing was ever in the background. We might say that his mind had no background, except perhaps that divine darkness out of which the divine love had called up every coloured creature one by one. He saw everything as dramatic, distinct from its setting, not all of a piece like a picture but in action like a play. A bird went by him like an arrow; something with a story and a purpose, though it was a purpose of life and not a purpose of death. A bush could stop him like a brigand; and indeed he

---

From Gilbert Keith Chesterton, *Saint Francis of Assisi* (New York: Doubleday Image Books, 1957), pp. 86–98.

was as ready to welcome the brigand as the bush.

In a word, we talk about a man who cannot see the wood for the trees. St. Francis was a man who did not want to see the wood for the trees. He wanted to see each tree as a separate and almost a sacred thing, being a child of God and therefore a brother or sister of man. But he did not want to stand against a piece of stage scenery used merely as a background, and inscribed in a general fashion: "Scene: a wood." In this sense we might say that he was too dramatic for the drama. The scenery would have come to life in his comedies; the walls would really have spoken like Snout the Tinker and the trees would really have come walking to Dunsinane. Everything would have been in the foreground; and in that sense in the footlights. Everything would be in every sense a character. This is the quality in which, as a poet, he is the very opposite of a pantheist. He did not call nature his mother; he called a particular donkey his brother or a particular sparrow his sister. If he had called a pelican his aunt or an elephant his uncle, as he might possibly have done, he would still have meant that they were particular creatures assigned by their Creator to particular places; not mere expressions of the evolutionary energy of things. That is where his mysticism is so close to the common sense of the child. A child has no difficulty about understanding that God made the dog and the cat; though he is well aware that the making of dogs and cats out of nothing if a mysterious process beyond his own imagination. But no child would understand what you meant if you mixed up the dog and the cat and everything else into one monster with myriad legs and called it nature. The child would resolutely refuse to make head or tail of any such animal. St. Francis was a mystic, but he believed in mysticism and not in mystification. As a mystic he was the mortal enemy of all those mystics who melt away the edges of things and dissolve an entity into its environment. He was a mystic of the daylight and the darkness; but not a mystic of the twilight. He was very contrary of that sort of oriental visionary who is only a mystic because he is too much of a sceptic to be a materialist. St. Francis was emphatically a realist, using the word realist in its much more real mediaeval sense. In this matter he really was akin to the best spirit of his age, which had just won its victory over the nominalism of the twelfth century. In this indeed there was something symbolic in the contemporary art and decoration of his period; as in the art of heraldry. The Franciscan birds and beasts were really rather like heraldic birds and beasts; not in the sense of being fabulous animals but in the sense of being treated as if they were facts, clear and positive and unaffected by the illusions of atmosphere and perspective. In that sense he did see a bird sable on a field azure or a sheep argent on a field vert. But the heraldry of humility was richer than the heraldry of pride; for it saw all these things that God had given as something more precious and unique than the blazonry that princes and peers had only given to themselves. Indeed out of the depths of that surrender it rose higher than the highest titles of the feudal age; than the laurel of Caesar or the Iron Crown of Lombardy. It is an example of extremes that meet, that the Little Poor Man, who had stripped himself of everything and named himself as nothing, took the same title that has been the wild vaunt of the vanity of the gorgeous Asiatic autocrat, and called himself the Brother of the Sun and Moon.

This quality, of something outstanding and even startling in things as St. Francis saw them, is here important as illustrating a character in his own life. As he saw all things dramatically, so he himself was always dramatic. We have to assume throughout, needless to say, that he was a poet and can only be understood as a poet. But he had one poetic privilege denied to most poets. In that respect indeed he might be called the one happy poet among all the unhappy poets of the world. He was a poet whose whole life was a poem. He was not so much a minstrel merely singing his own songs as a dramatist capable of acting the whole of his own play. The things he said were more imaginative than the things he wrote. The things he did were more imaginative than the things he said. His whole course through life was a series of scenes in which he had a sort of perpetual luck in bringing things to a beautiful crisis. To talk about the art of living has come to sound rather artificial than artistic. But St. Francis did in a definite sense make the very act of living an art, though it was an unpremeditated art. Many of his acts will seem grotesque and puzzling to a rationalistic taste. But they were always acts and not explanations; and they always meant what he meant them to mean. The amazing vividness with which he stamped himself on the memory and imagination of mankind is very largely due to the fact that he was seen again and again under such dramatic conditions. From the moment when he rent his robes and flung them at his father's feet to the moment when he stretched himself in death on the bare earth in the pattern of the cross, his life was made up of these unconscious attitudes and unhesitating gestures. It would be easy to fill page after page with examples; but I will here pursue the method found convenient everywhere in this short sketch, and take one typical example, dwelling on it with a little more detail than would be possible in a catalogue, in the hope of making the meaning more clear. The example taken here occurred in the last days of his life, but it refers back in a rather curious fashion to the first; and rounds off the remarkable unity of that romance of religion.

The phrase about his brotherhood with the sun and moon, and with the water and the fire, occurs of course in his famous poem called the Canticle of the Creatures or the Canticle of the Sun. He sang it wandering in the meadows in the sunnier season of his own career, when he was pouring upwards into the sky all the passions of a poet. It is a supremely characteristic work, and much of St. Francis could be reconstructed from that work alone. Though in some ways the thing is as simple and straightforward as a ballad, there is a delicate instinct of differentiation in it. Notice, for instance, the sense of sex in inanimate things, which goes far beyond the arbitrary genders of a grammar. It was not for nothing that he called fire his brother, fierce and gay and strong, and water his sister, pure and clear and inviolate. Remember that St. Francis was neither encumbered nor assisted by all that Greek and Roman polytheism turned into allegory, which has been to European poetry often an inspiration, too often a convention. Whether he gained or lost by his contempt of learning, it never occurred to him to connect Neptune and the nymphs with the water or Vulcan and the Cyclops with the flame. This point exactly illustrates what has already been suggested; that, so far from being a revival of paganism, the Franciscan renascence was a sort of fresh start and first awakening after a forgetfulness of paganism. Certainly it is responsible for a certain freshness in the thing itself. Anyhow St. Francis was, as it were, the founder of a new folklore; but he could distinguish his mermaids from her mermen and his witches from his wizards. In short, he had to make his own mythology; but he knew at a glance the goddesses from the gods. This fanciful instinct for the sexes is not the only example of an imaginative instinct of the kind. There is just the same quaint felicity in the fact that he singles out the sun with a slightly more courtly title besides that of brother; a phrase that one king might use of another, corresponding to "Monsieur notre frère." It is like a faint half ironic shadow of the shining primacy that it had held in the pagan heavens. A bishop is said to have complained of a Non-conformist saying Paul instead of Saint Paul; and to have added, "He might at least have called him Mr. Paul." So St. Francis is free of all obligation to cry out in praise or terror of the Lord God Apollo, but in his new nursery heavens, he salutes him as Mr. Sun. Those are the things in which he has a sort of inspired infancy, only to be paralleled in nursery tales. Something of the same hazy but healthy awe makes the story of Br'er Fox and Br'er Rabbit refer respectfully to Mr. Man.

This poem, full of the mirth of youth and the memories of childhood, runs through his whole life like a refrain, and scraps of it turn up continually in the ordinary habit of his talk. Perhaps the the last appearance of its special language was in an incident that has always seemed to me intensely impressive, and is at any rate very illustrative of the great manner and gesture of which I

speak. Impressions of that kind are a matter of imagination and
in that sense of taste. It is idle to argue about them; for it is the
whole point of them that they have passed beyond words; and
even when they use words, seem to be completed by some ritual
movement like a blessing or a blow. So, in a supreme example,
there is something far past all exposition, something like the
sweeping movement and mighty shadow of a hand, darkening
even the darkness of Gethsemane; "Sleep on now, and take your
rest. . . ." Yet there are people who have started to paraphrase
and expand the story of the Passion.

St. Francis was a dying man. We might say he was an old man,
at the time this typical incident occurred; but in fact he was only
prematurely old; for he was not fifty when he died, worn out with
his fighting and fasting life. But when he came down from the
awful asceticism and more awful revelation of Alverno, he was a
broken man. As will be apparent when these events are touched
on in their turn, it was not only sickness and bodily decay that
may well have darkened his life; he had been recently disappointed in his main mission to end the Crusades by the conversion of Islam; he had been still more disappointed by the signs
of compromise and a more political or practical spirit in his own
order; he had spent his last energies in protest. At this point he
was told that he was going blind. If the faintest hint has been
given here of what St. Francis felt about the glory and pageantry
of earth and sky, about the heraldic shape and colour and symbolism of birds and beasts and flowers, some notion may be formed
of what it meant to him to go blind. Yet the remedy might well
have seemed worse than the disease. The remedy, admittedly an
uncertain remedy, was to cauterise the eye, and that without any
anaesthetic. In other words it was to burn his living eyeballs with
a red-hot iron. Many of the tortures of martyrdom, which he
enviewed in martyrology and sought vainly in Syria, can have
been no worse. When they took the brand from the furnace, he
rose as with an urbane gesture and spoke as to an invisible presence: "Brother Fire, God made you beautiful and strong and

useful; I pray you be courteous with me."

If there be any such thing as the art of life, it seems to me that such a moment was one of its masterpieces. Not to many poets has it been given to remember their own poetry at such a moment, still less to live one of their own poems. Even William Blake would have been disconcerted if, while he was rereading the noble lines, "Tiger, tiger, burning bright," a real large live Bengal tiger had put his head in at the window of the cottage in Felpham, evidently with every intention of biting his head off. He might have wavered before politely saluting it, above all by calmly completing the recitation of the poem to the quadruped to whom it was dedicated. Shelley, when he wished to be a cloud or a leaf carried before the wind, might have been mildly surprised to find himself turning slowly head over heels in mid-air a thousand feet above the sea. Even Keats, knowing that his hold on life was a frail one, might have been disturbed to discover that the true, the blushful Hippocrene of which he had just partaken freely had indeed contained a drug, which really ensured that he should cease upon the midnight with no pain. For Francis there was no drug; and for Francis there was plenty of pain. But his first thought was one of his first fancies from the songs of his youth. He remembered the time when a flame was a flower, only the most glorious and gaily coloured of the flowers in the garden of God; and when that shining thing returned to him in the shape of an instrument of torture, he hailed it from afar like an old friend, calling it by the nickname which might most truly be called its Christian name.

That is only one incident out of a life of such incidents; and I have selected it partly because it shows what is meant here by that shadow of gesture there is in all his words, the dramatic gesture of the south; and partly because its special reference to courtesy covers the next fact to be noted. The popular instinct of St. Francis, and his perpetual preoccupation with the idea of brotherhood, will be entirely misunderstood if it is understood in the sense of what is often called camaraderie; the backslapping sort of brotherhood. Frequently from the enemies and too frequently from the friends of the democratic ideal, there has come a notion that this note is necessary to that ideal. It is assumed that equality means all men being equally uncivil, whereas it obviously ought to mean all men being equally civil. Such people have forgotten the very meaning and derivation of the word civility, if they do not see that to be uncivil is to be uncivic. But anyhow that was not the equality which Francis of Assisi encouraged; but an equality of the opposite kind; it was a camaraderie actually founded on courtesy.

Even in that fairy borderland of his mere fancies about flowers and animals and even inanimate things, he retained this permanent posture of a sort of deference. A friend of mine said that somebody was the sort of man who apologises to the cat. St. Francis really would have apologised to the cat. When he was about to preach in a wood full of the chatter of birds, he said, with a gentle gesture, "Little sisters, if you have now had your say, it is time that I also should be heard." And all the birds were silent; as I for one can very easily believe. In deference to my special design of making matters intelligible to average modernity, I have treated separately the subject of the miraculous powers that St. Francis most certainly possessed. But even apart from any miraculous powers, men of that magnetic sort, with that intense interest in animals, often have an extraordinary power over them. St. Francis's power was always exercised with this elaborate politeness. Much of it was doubtless a sort of symbolic joke, a pious pantomime intended to convey the vital distinction in his divine mission, that he not only loved but reverenced God in all his creatures. In this sense he had the air not only of apologising to the cat or to the birds, but of apologising to a chair for sitting on it or to a table for sitting down at it. Any one who had followed him through life merely to laugh at him, as a sort of lovable lunatic, might easily have had an impression as of a lunatic who bowed to every post or took off his hat to every tree. This was all a part of his instinct for imaginative gesture. He taught the world a large part of its lesson by a sort of divine dumb alphabet. But if there was this ceremonial element even in lighter or lesser matters, its significance became far more serious in the serious work of his life, which was an appeal to humanity, or rather to human beings.

I have said that St. Francis deliberately did not see the wood for the trees. It is even more true that he deliberately did not see the mob for the men. What distinguishes this very genuine democrat from any mere demagogue is that he never either deceived or was deceived by the illusion of mass-suggestion. Whatever his taste in monsters, he never saw before him a many-headed beast. He only saw the image of God multiplied but never monotonous. To him a man was always a man and did not disappear in a dense crowd any more than in a desert. He honoured all men; that is, he not only loved but respected them all. What gave him his extraordinary personal power was this: that from the Pope to the beggar, from the sultan of Syria in his pavilion to the ragged robbers crawling out of the wood, there was never a man who looked into those brown burning eyes without being certain that Francis Bernardone was really interested in him; in his own inner individual life from the cradle to the grave; that he himself was being valued and taken seriously, and not merely added to the spoils of some social policy or the names in some clerical document. Now for this particular moral and religious idea there is no external expression except courtesy. Exhortation does not express it, for it is not mere abstract enthusiasm; beneficence does not express it, for it is not mere pity. It can only be conveyed by a certain grand manner which may be called good manners. We may say if we like that St. Francis, in the bare and barren simplicity of his life, had clung to one rage of luxury; the manners of a court. But whereas in a court there is one king and a hundred courtiers, in this story there was one courtier, moving among a hundred kings. For he treated the whole mob of men as a mob of kings. And this was really and truly the only attitude that will appeal to that part of man to which he wished to appeal. It cannot be done by giving gold or even bread; for it is a proverb that any reveller may fling largesse in mere scorn. It cannot even be done by giving time and attention; for any number of philanthropists and benevolent bureaucrats do such work with a scorn far more cold and horrible in their hearts. No plans or proposals or efficient rearrangements will give back to a broken man his self-respect and sense of speaking with an equal. One gesture will do it.

With that gesture Francis of Assisi moved among men; and it was soon found to have something in it of magic and to act, in a double sense, like a charm. But it must always be conceived as a completely natural gesture; for indeed it was almost a gesture of apology. He must be imagined as moving thus swiftly through the world with a sort of impetuous politeness; almost like the movement of a man who stumbles on one knee half in haste and half in obeisance. The eager face under the brown hood was that of a man always going somewhere, as if he followed as well as watched the flight of the birds. And this sense of motion is indeed the meaning of the whole revolution that he made; for the work that has now to be described was of the nature of an earthquake or a volcano, an explosion that drove outwards with dynamic energy the forces stored up by ten centuries in the monastic fortress or arsenal and scattered all its riches recklessly to the ends of the earth. In a better sense than the antithesis commonly conveys, it is true to say that what St. Benedict had stored St. Francis scattered; but in the world of spiritual things what had been stored into the barns like grain was scattered over the world as seed. The servants of God who had been a besieged garrison became a marching army; the ways of the world were filled as with thunder with the trampling of their feet and far ahead of that ever swelling host went a man singing; as simply as he had sung that morning in the winter woods, where he walked alone.

The Canticle of Brother Sun

Most High, omnipotent, good Lord
To you alone belong praise and glory,
Honor, and blessing.
No man is worthy to breathe thy name.

Be praised, my Lord, for all your creatures.

In the first place for the blessed Brother Sun,
who gives us the day and enlightens us through you.
He is beautiful and radiant with his great splendor,
Giving witness of thee, Most Omnipotent One.

Be praised, my Lord, for Sister Moon and the stars
Formed by you so bright, precious, and beautiful.

Be praised, my Lord, for Brother Wind
And the airy skies, so cloudy and serene;
For every weather, be praised, for it is life-giving.

Translated from the Italian by the editor.

Be praised, my Lord, for Sister Water,
So necessary yet so humble, precious, and chaste.

Be praised, my Lord, for Brother Fire,
Who lights up the night.
He is beautiful and carefree, robust, and fierce.

Be praised, my Lord, for our sister, Mother Earth,
Who nourishes and watches us
While bringing forth abundance of fruits with colored flowers
And herbs.

Be praised, my Lord, for those who pardon through your love
And bear weakness and trial.
Blessed are those who endure in peace,
For they will be crowned by you, Most High.

Be praised, my Lord, for our sister, Bodily Death,
Whom no living man can escape.
Woe to those who die in sin.
Blessed are those who discover thy holy will.
The second death will do them no harm.

Praise and bless my Lord.
Render thanks.
Serve him with great humility.

                                              Amen.

Selections From the Early Life of the Saint

He overflowed with a spirit of love not only for men who suffered but also for dumb animals, reptiles, birds, and any other creature with and without consciousness. Above all, he loved little lambs with a special affection and love, for they showed forth the humility of our Lord Jesus Christ, since the Scriptures used the image of a lamb in describing him. Saint Francis would more readily embrace those animals in which he found some similarity with our Lord.

A certain nobleman from Siena once sent him a pheasant when he was sick. He was delighted with the gift, not because he had intention of eating it but because he could rejoice in its beauty and thus intensify his love for the Creator. He used to say to the pheasant, "Praised be our Creator, Brother Pheasant."

Near the cell of the saint at Saint Mary of the Angels, a cicada used to perch in a tree and chirp out all day long. At times the blessed father would hold out his hand and call it to him, "Come

---

Adapted and translated by the editor from the *Vita Prima* and *Vita Secunda* of Thomas of Celano.

to me, Sister Cicada." And she would fly right to him as if endowed with reason.

Even toward little worms, he had a great sense of love, for he had read in the Scriptures concerning our Lord, "I am a worm and no man."

When he would come on a vast field of flowers, he would preach to them and exhort them to praise God as if they could understand his words. He would likewise exhort cornfields, vineyards, stones, fields, springs of water, green plants in gardens, earth, fire, and water to a praise and love for the Creator. In short, he called all creatures by the name of *brother* and, in a manner that few can understand, he saw the simple things of creation with the eye of one whose heart had already attained to the blessed liberty of the children of God.

When the brothers were cutting wood, he would forbid them to cut down the whole tree so that it might grow up again. He also ordered the gardeners not to dig up the edges of the gardens so that wild flowers and green grasses could grow and glorify the Father of all things. In the same vein, he would order gardeners always to leave aside a plot for sweet-smelling flowers and herbs so that men would be reminded of the sweetness of the Lord. He picked up worms so they would not be trampled on and had honey and wine set out for the bees in the winter season. He called by the name of *brother* all animals, although he himself was more partial to the gentle animals.

Selections from the Fioretti

How Saint Francis was Puzzled About His Life: Should He Pray Exclusively or Also Give Time to Preaching?

The humble servant of God, Saint Francis, a short time after his conversion already had many companions and associates in his order. He began to worry at this point about his own life: should he retire to devote himself to prayer or also spend time in preaching? Above all, he wanted to know what the will of God was in this matter. Since he was so humble, he trusted neither his own judgment nor his own prayers but sought out the prayerful advice of others. So he called Brother Masseo one day and said to him, "Go to Sister Clare and ask her along with some of her more spiritual sisters to devoutly pray to God so that it might please him to show me what to do: to pray or to devote some time to preaching. Then to to Brother Silvestro and ask him to do the same."

This Brother Silvestro was the one who was Signor Silvestro in the world who had seen the cross of gold coming from the

_____

Translated from the Italian by the editor.

mouth of Saint Francis and extending to the sky and to the horizons of the world. This same Brother Silvestro was of such holiness that whatever he asked of God was granted. He often spoke with God, and for this reason Saint Francis had much confidence in him.

So Brother Masseo went first to Sister Clare and then to Brother Silvestro just as Saint Francis had ordered. Brother Silvestro fell immediately into prayer when he heard the request. Having prayed a bit, he said to Brother Masseo, "God says that Saint Francis should know this: God has called him into this state not only for himself but also for the sake of many who need salvation." Brother Masseo then went to Saint Clare to ask her what response she had received from her prayer. She said that she and her companion had received the same message that he had already heard from Brother Silvestro.

With this information Brother Masseo returned to Saint Francis, who received him with great love, washing his feet and fixing something for him to eat. After he had eaten, Francis called Masseo into a wooded area, knelt before him, uncovered his head, crossed his arms, and asked, "What does the Lord Jesus Christ commend me to do?" Brother Masseo then told him what Brother Silvestro, Sister Clare, and her spiritual sisters had all said in having Christ reveal his will about Francis's life: "You should go into the world and preach, for you have been called not for yourself alone but for the souls of many."

When Saint Francis had heard this, he knew it to be the will of Christ. So he rose up right away and with the greatest fervor he said, "Let us go in the name of God." And Brother Masseo and Brother Agnolo, both holy men, accompanied him. And going under the impetus of the Spirit, taking no pause or rest, they arrived at the castle of Cannara.

Saint Francis began to preach after warning the swallows in the place to keep silent and not to sing until he had finished his sermon. The birds obeyed him, and he preached with such fervor that the men and women of the castle wished to follow him and simply abandon the castle. But Saint Francis would not permit this. He said to them, "Do not act hastily. Do not leave this castle. I will set up a way of life that you may follow for the salvation of your souls." He was thinking of his third order for the universal salvation of souls. Then, leaving them consoled and well disposed, he took the road from Cannara to Bevagno.

Passing along the road, he raised his eyes and saw some trees along the side of the path. In the trees there was a vast, almost infinite, flock of birds. Saint Francis was struck by the fine sight and said to his companions, "You wait here on the road. I'm going over there and preach to my sisters, the birds." And he went into the field and began to preach to the birds who were on the ground. Almost immediately the birds who were in the trees came and joined the others. They stayed absolutely still, while Saint Francis spoke to them. They did not fly off until he had blessed them with the sign of the cross. And, according to what Brother Masseo told Brother Jacopo da Massa, even when Saint Francis moved among them and brushed them with the hem of his garment, none of them flew off or moved.

The substance of the sermon of Saint Francis was this:

"My little Sisters Birds, you are such beloved by God, your creator, and in every place you should praise him with your song. Remember that he has doubly and even triply dressed you, and you can go where you wish. He saved your species in the ark of Noah so that you would not be lost to the world. You should also be thankful for the sustenance of the air, which God has given you as your province. Beyond that, you do not have to plant or harvest. God gives you food to eat and provides springs and rivers for when you are thirsty; there are hills and valleys for your refuge and trees to build your nests. You do not have to sew or weave, for God gives you and your offspring ample clothing. So —love your creator, for he has done so much for you. Finally, my little sisters, beware of the sin of ingratitude. Be ready always to praise and thank God."

When Saint Francis had finished, the birds began to open their beaks, extend their wings, stretch their necks, and bob their heads to show that they understood; by their songs and trills they showed that they received the words with great love. And Saint Francis, right in the midst of them, was happy and filled with joy. Many were struck by the vast number of the birds, their different plumage, their attention and carefreeness around him. So the saint, together with the birds, devoutly praised the Creator.

Finally, when he had finished, Saint Francis made the sign of the cross over them and gave them permission to fly off. All the birds, in a single flight, took off into the sky with marvelous song. When Francis made a second sign of the cross, the birds divided into four parts, flying off to the east and west, to the north and south, and each flock kept singing in a marvelous manner. All this symbolized that just as Saint Francis, the standard-bearer of the cross of Christ, blessed the birds and had them divided into four parts of the world, so the preaching of the cross of Christ, newly restored by Saint Francis, would be carried by him and his brothers into every part of the world. These brothers, like the birds of the air, were to have nothing but to depend for everything in this world on the providence of God.

To the praise of Christ. Amen.

[Chapter XVI]

How Saint Francis Freed the City of Gubbio of a Ravenous Wolf

While Saint Francis was staying in the town of Gubbio, there appeared a huge wolf. It was so ferocious and terrible that it devoured not only animals but also men. The citizens of the town were so terrified that they always went out fully armed as if ready to go to war. But, despite this, they were helpless, especially when a single man met the wolf. Because of their fear, nobody would even venture out of the house.

Because of this, Saint Francis (who felt great pity for the people) made up his mind to go and find the wolf, even though everyone told him not to. Still, making the sign of the cross, he went out one day with his companions, putting his trust in God.

His companions hung back, but Saint Francis took the road leading to the place where the wolf was often found. A number of people followed in order to see a miracle, and when the open-mouthed wolf approached Saint Francis, the saint made the sign of the cross over the wolf and called out to him, "Come to me, Brother Wolf, and I order you, in the name of Christ, neither to harm me nor the others."

Incredible as it seems, the moment Saint Francis made the sign of the cross, the wolf closed his mouth and stopped dead in his tracks. When he heard the order, he came meekly to the feet of Saint Francis and laid down.

Then Saint Francis spoke to him, "Brother Wolf, you have done much damage in these parts and committed great crimes by maiming and killing God's creatures without his permission. You haven't stopped at this but also maimed and killed men who are made in the likeness of God. You ought to be treated like a robber and a murderer and handed over to the hangman. The people hate and curse you, and this land is an enemy to you. But, Brother Wolf, I want to make peace between you and these people. If you will stop harming them, they, in turn, will forgive you, and neither men nor dogs will pester you in the future."

When Saint Francis said this, the wolf showed his agreement with the words of the saint by signaling with his body and tail and ears and with a nod of his head showed his compliance. Then Saint Francis said, "Brother Wolf, since you are ready to make peace and keep your word, I promise that these people will give you enough to eat during your life so that you need not starve. I understand that you did these evil things because of hunger. Since I have begged this favor, Brother Wolf, you must promise me to harm neither animal nor man. Do you promise this?" And the wolf, with a nod of his head, promised.

Then Saint Francis said, "Brother Wolf, I want you to give me a sign that you have promised so that I can have faith in you. Saint Francis put out his hand as a sign of their pact and the wolf lifted its paw and tamely put it in the hand of Saint Francis, giving the best sign of faith that he could. Then Saint Francis said, "Brother Wolf, I command you in the name of Jesus Christ to come with me without fear, and we can go and make peace in the name of God." And the wolf obediently followed him as a meek lamb would.

The citizens of the town were stupefied. The news spread everywhere, and in a moment the people—young and old, men and women—lined the piazza to see Saint Francis with the wolf. When Saint Francis saw the crowd, he stepped forward and began to preach to them. He told them that God permitted such evils because of sinfulness and that they should fear the pain of eternal damnation more than a wolf, who can only kill their bodies. He said that they should fear the opening of the jaws of hell more than the jaws of a simple animal. "Be converted, beloved of God, and do penance for your sins, and God will free you from the wolf today and the gates of hell tomorrow."

When he had finished his talk, Saint Francis said, "Listen to me, my brothers. Brother Wolf, who is here before you, has promised and sworn peace with you now and in the future; he will do you no harm if you will give him a bit to eat. And I promise that he will keep his end of the bargain." The people unanimously promised to feed him daily. Then Saint Francis said to the wolf, "And you, Brother Wolf, do you promise to keep the peace and not harm the animals or men or any other creature?" And the wolf, kneeling down with head bowed, made signs with his tail and ears to indicate that he wished to keep the pact.

Saint Francis said, "Brother Wolf, I want you to make the sign of agreement that you made outside the city gate here among the people so that you will show that you will not betray the pact that I have made in your name." And the wolf put his right paw in the hand of Saint Francis. With this, and because of all the other things they had seen, the people began to praise God in the heavens for sending them Saint Francis and for freeing them from the ravages of the once wild wolf.

After this the wolf lived in Gubbio for two years. He went daily from house to house without harm or being harmed. The people fed him and he was such a familiar sight that the dogs didn't even bark at him. Finally, after two years, Brother Wolf died of old age. The people mourned him, because he had been a familiar sight among them and was a constant reminder of the virtue and holiness of Saint Francis.

To the praise of Christ. Amen.

[Chapter XXI]

How a Young Man Gave Some Doves To Saint Francis, and They Would Not Leave Without The Saint's Permission

Once a young man had a lot of doves and was on his way to sell them. Saint Francis met him on the road. Saint Francis always felt a great pity for weak animals, and he looked at the poor doves with eyes filled with compassion. He said to the boy, "My good young man, please give me those doves, for they are sweet and innocent birds which Sacred Scripture likens to humble, chaste, and faithful souls. I do not want them to fall into the hands of cruel men who will kill them." The young boy, under the impulse of God, handed them right over to the saint, who took them into his lap and began to speak to them ever so sweetly: "Oh, my little Sisters Doves. You are so innocent, chaste, and simple. Why did you allow yourself to get trapped? I want you to escape death, so I'm going to make you a nest so that you may have other little ones and multiply just as God your Creator has willed." And so he went off and made some nests, and they began to live there, lay eggs, and produce little ones, and the brothers could watch all this. They were so tame around Saint Francis and the other brothers that they seemed like little chickens that had been raised from infancy. They would not go away unless Saint Francis gave them a blessing and a permission to depart.

To the young boy who had given Saint Francis the doves, he said, "My Son, you will be a brother in this order one day, and you will serve Jesus Christ most worthily." And so it happened. The boy became a friar and lived in the order in great sanctity.

In the praise of Christ. Amen.

[Chapter XXII]

How Saint Anthony Preached to the Fish Near Rimini

The Blessed Christ once wished to show forth the sanctity of his most faithful servant, Saint Anthony of Padua, and also demonstrate how His preached word and holy doctrine should also be heard by dumb animals. To this end, Saint Anthony once preached about the foolishness of heretics to fish, just as, in ancient times, the ignorance of Balaam was announced through the mouth of an ass, as the Old Testament tells us.

Saint Anthony was once in Rimini, where there were many heretics. He wanted to bring them to the true light of the faith and to set them on the path of truth. So for many days he was in the town preaching about Christ and explaining the Holy Scriptures. But the heretics were not only not convinced but also so hardened and obstinate that they would not even listen to him.

So Saint Anthony, inspired by God, left the town and went to the banks of the river where it meets the sea and began, in a loud voice, to preach to the fish, "Hear the word of the Lord, you fish of the river and the sea, for the infidels will not!"

As soon as he began to speak, there arose a great school of fish that were little, middle sized, and great. Nobody had ever seen such a multitude before. They all stood at attention with their heads out of the water, facing Saint Anthony. The smallest were in the first rows, then the medium sized, and finally, in the deeper water, the very largest of the fish of the sea.

Once they were standing in perfect order and seemed ready to listen, Saint Anthony began to preach in the most solemn of tones:

"My Brothers Fish, you are obliged, to the extent you are able, to render thanks to your creator, who has given you such a noble element to dwell in. For, according to your need, you have both sweet and salt water. There are many places for you to hide from the storms, and there is abundant food for you to eat. God, your creator, gave you the commandment to increase and multiply when he made you, and he extended a blessing over you. When the great flood came, God willed that you be saved, while all other animals were lost. He gave you fins so that you could travel wherever you wished. To you it was granted to save the prophet Jonah and after three days to throw him up on the shore. You offered the coin of tribute to our Lord Jesus Christ, poor man that he was, so he could pay the tax. You were food for our Lord Jesus Christ, the Eternal King, both before and after his resurrection. For these, and for many other reasons, you should praise and give glory to God."

While these words and admonitions were spoken by Saint Anthony, the fish opened their mouths and inclined their heads to show that they were praising God. Saint Anthony, seeing the great reverence of the fish toward the Creator, was exalted in spirit and cried out with a loud voice, "Blessed be the Eternal God, for the fish of the sea praise him more than errant men; the animals hear his Word with more understanding than unfaithful creatures of reason."

The more Saint Anthony spoke, the greater was the school of fish. None left the spot where he was speaking. Soon the people of the town heard what was happening, and they came out to see the event, and among their number were the aforementioned

heretics. When they saw this miraculous event, they threw themselves at the feet of the saint and begged him to preach to them.

So Saint Anthony began to preach the Catholic faith to the
people, and so great was his impact that many returned to the
true faith. Those who had always been faithful were strengthened
and comforted in their faith. After this all had happened, Saint
Anthony sent the fish off with the blessing of God, and the people
likewise returned to their homes. Saint Anthony stayed on in the
town for some time, preaching and harvesting much spiritual
fruit.

In the praise of Christ. Amen.

[Chapter XL]

The Historical Roots of Our Ecological Crisis

A conversation with Aldous Huxley not infrequently put one at the receiving end of an unforgettable monologue. About a year before his lamented death he was discoursing on a favorite topic: Man's unnatural treatment of nature and its sad results. To illustrate his point he told how, during the previous summer, he had returned to a little valley in England where he had spent many happy months as a child. Once it had been composed of delightful grassy glades; now it was becoming overgrown with unsightly brush because the rabbits that formerly kept such growth under control had largely succumbed to a disease, myxomatosis, that was deliberately introduced by local farmers to reduce the rabbits' destruction of crops. Being something of a Philistine, I could be silent no longer, even in the interests of great rhetoric. I interrupted to point out that the rabbit itself had been brought as a domestic animal to England in 1176, presumably to improve the protein diet of the peasantry.

All forms of life modify their contexts. The most spectacular and benign instance is doubtless the coral polyp. By serving its

Lynn White, Jr., "The Historical Roots of Our Ecological Crisis," *Science*, March 10, 1967, pp. 1203–7.

81

own ends, it has created a vast undersea world favorable to thousands of other kinds of animals and plants. Ever since man became a numerous species he has affected his environment notably. The hypothesis that his fire-drive method of hunting created the world's great grasslands and helped to exterminate the monster mammals of the Pleistocene from much of the globe is plausible, if not proved. For 6 millennia at least, the banks of the lower Nile have been a human artifact rather than the swampy African jungle which nature, apart from man, would have made it. The Aswan Dam, flooding 5000 square miles, is only the latest stage in a long process. In many regions terracing or irrigation, overgrazing, the cutting of forests by Romans to build ships to fight Carthaginians or by Crusaders to solve the logistics problems of their expeditions, have profoundly changed some ecologies. Observation that the French landscape falls into two basic types, the open fields of the north and the *bocage* of the south and west, inspired Marc Bloch to undertake his classic study of medieval agricultural methods. Quite unintentionally, changes in human ways often affect nonhuman nature. It has been noted, for example, that the advent of the automobile eliminated huge flocks of sparrow that once fed on the horse manure littering every street.

The history of ecologic change is still so rudimentary that we know little about what really happened, or what the results were. The extinction of the European aurochs as late as 1627 would seem to have been a simple case of overenthusiastic hunting. On more intricate matters it often is impossible to find solid information. For a thousand years or more the Frisians and Hollanders have been pushing back the North Sea, and the process is culminating in our own time in the reclamation of the Zuider Zee. What, if any, species of animals, birds, fish, shore life, or plants have died out in the process? In their epic combat with Neptune have the Netherlanders overlooked ecological values in such a way that the quality of human life in the Netherlands has suffered? I cannot discover that the questions have ever been asked, much less answered.

People, then, have often been a dynamic element in their own environment, but in the present state of historical scholarship we usually do not know exactly when, where, or with what effects man-induced changes came. As we enter the last third of the 20th century, however, concern for the problem of ecological backlash is mounting feverishly. Natural science, conceived as the effort to understand the nature of things, had flourished in several eras and among several peoples. Similarly there had been an age-old accumulation of technological skills, sometimes growing rapidly, sometimes slowly. But it was not until about four generations ago that Western Europe and North America arranged a marriage between science and technology, a union of the theoretical and the empirical approaches to our natural environment. The emergence in widespread practice of the Baconian creed that scientific knowledge means technological power over nature can scarcely be dated before about 1850, save in the chemical industries, where it is anticipated in the 18th century. Its acceptance as a normal pattern of action may mark the greatest event in human history since the invention of agriculture, and perhaps in nonhuman terrestrial history as well.

Almost at once the new situation forced the crystallization of the novel concept of ecology; indeed, the word *ecology* first appeared in the English language in 1873. Today, less than a century later, the impact of our race upon the environment has so increased in force that it has changed in essence. When the first cannons were fired, in the early 14th century, they affected ecology by sending workers scrambling to the forests and mountains for more potash, sulfur, iron ore, and charcoal, with some resulting erosion and deforestation. Hydrogen bombs are of a different order: a war fought with them might alter the genetics of all life on this planet. By 1285 London had a smog problem arising from the burning of soft coal, but our present combustion of fossil fuels threatens to change the chemistry of the globe's atmosphere as a whole, with consequences which we are only beginning to guess. With the population explosion, the carcinoma of planless urbanism, the now geological deposits of sewage and garbage, surely no creature other than man has ever managed to foul its nest in such short order.

There are many calls to action, but specific proposals, however worthy as individual items, seem too partial, palliative, negative: ban the bomb, tear down the billboards, give the Hindus contraceptives, and tell them to eat their sacred cows. The simplest solution to any suspect change is, of course, to stop it, or, better yet, to revert to a romanticized past: make those ugly gasoline stations look like Anne Hathaway's cottage or (in the Far West) like ghost-town saloons. The "wilderness area" mentality invariably advocates deep-freezing an ecology, whether San Gimignano or the High Sierra, as it was before the first Kleenex was dropped. But neither atavism nor prettification will cope with the ecologic crisis of our time.

What shall we do? No one yet knows. Unless we think about fundamentals, our specific measures may produce new backlashes more serious than those they are designed to remedy.

As a beginning we should try to clarify our thinking by looking, in some historical depth, at the presuppositions that underlie modern technology and science. Science was traditionally aristocratic, speculative, intellectual in intent; technology was lower-class, empirical, action-oriented. The quite sudden fusion of these two, towards the middle of the 19th century, is surely related to the slightly prior and contemporary democratic revolutions which, by reducing social barriers, tended to assert a functional unity of brain and hand. Our ecologic crisis is the product of an emerging, entirely novel, democratic culture. The issue is whether a democratized world can survive its own implications. Presumably we cannot unless we rethink our axioms.

THE WESTERN TRADITIONS OF TECHNOLOGY AND SCIENCE

One thing is so certain that it seems stupid to verbalize it: both modern technology and modern science are distinctively *Occiden-*

tal. Our technology has absorbed elements from all over the world, notably from China; yet everywhere today, whether in Japan or in Nigeria, successful technology is Western. Our science is the heir to all the sciences of the past, especially perhaps to the work of the great Islamic scientists of the Middle Ages, who so often outdid the ancient Greeks in skill and perspicacity: al-Razi in medicine, for example; or ibn-al-Haytham in optics; or Omar Khayyam in mathematics. Indeed, not a few works of such geniuses seem to have vanished in the original Arabic and to survive only in medieval Latin translations that helped to lay the foundations for later Western developments. Today, around the globe, all significant science is Western in style and method, whatever the pigmentation or language of the scientists.

A second pair of facts is less well recognized because they result from quite recent historical scholarship. The leadership of the West, both in technology and in science, is far older than the so-called Industrial Revolution of the 18th century. These terms are in fact outmoded and obscure the true nature of what they try to describe—significant stages in two long and separate developments. By A.D. 1000 at the latest—and perhaps, feebly, as much as 200 years earlier—the West began to apply water power to industrial processes other than milling grain. This was followed in the late 12th century by the harnessing of wind power. From simply beginning, but with remarkable consistency of style, the West rapidly expanded its skills in the development of power machinery, labor-saving devices, and automation. Those who doubt should contemplate that most monumental achievement in the history of automation: the weight-driven mechanical clock, which appeared in two forms in the early 14th century. Not in craftsmanship but in basic technological capacity, the Latin West of the later Middle Ages far outstripped its elaborate, sophisticated, and aesthetically magnificent sister cultures, Byzantium and Islam. In 1444 a great Greek ecclesiastic, Bessarion, who had gone to Italy, wrote a letter to a prince in Greece. He is amazed by the superiority of Western ships, arms, textiles, glass. But above all he is astonished by the spectacle of waterwheels sawing timbers and pumping the bellows of blast furnaces. Clearly he had seen nothing of the sort in the Near East.

By the end of the 15th century the technological superiority of Europe was such that its small, mutually hostile nations could spill out over all the rest of the world, conquering, looting, and colonizing. The symbol of this technological superiority is the fact that Portugal, one of the weakest states of the Occident, was able to become, and to remain for a century, mistress of the East Indies. And we must remember that the technology of Vasco da Gamma and Albuquerque was built by pure empiricism, drawing remarkable little support or inspiration from science.

In the present-day vernacular understanding, modern science is supposed to have begun in 1543, when both Copernicus and Vesalius published their great works. It is no derogation of their accomplishments, however, to point out that such structures as the *Fabrica* and the *De revolutionibus* do not appear overnight. The distinctive Western tradition of science, in fact, began in the late 11th century with a massive movement of translation of Arabic and Greek scientific works into Latin. A few notable books— Theophrastus, for example—escaped the West's avid new appetite for science, but within less than 200 years effectively the entire corpus of Greek and Muslim science was available in Latin, and was being eagerly read and criticized in the new European universities. Out of criticism arose new observation, speculation, and increasing distrust of ancient authorities. By the late 13th century Europe had seized global scientific leadership from the faltering hands of Islam. It would be as absurd to deny the profound originality of Newton, Galileo, or Copernicus as to deny that of the 14th century scholastic scientists like Buridan or Oresme on whose work they built. Before the 11th century, science scarcely existed in the Latin West, even in Roman times. From the 11th century onward, the scientific sector of Occidental culture has increased in a steady crescendo.

Since both our technological and our scientific movements got their start, acquired their character, and achieved world dominance in the Middle Ages, it would seem that we cannot understand their nature or their present impact upon ecology without examining fundamental medieval assumptions and developments.

MEDIEVAL VIEW OF MAN AND NATURE

Until recently, agriculture has been the chief occupation even in "advanced" societies; hence, any change in methods of tillage has much importance. Early plows, drawn by two oxen, did not normally turn the sod but merely scratched it. Thus, cross-plowing was needed and fields tended to be squarish. In the fairly light soils and semi-arid climates of the Near East and Mediterranean, this worked well. But such a plow was inappropriate to the wet climate and often sticky soils of northern Europe. By the latter part of the 7th century after Christ, however, following obscure beginnings, certain northern peasants were using an entirely new kind of plow, equipped with a vertical knife to cut the line of the furrow, a horizontal share to slice under the sod, and a moldboard to turn it over. The friction of this plow with the soil was so great that it normally required not two but eight oxen. It attacked the land with such violence that cross-plowing was not needed, and fields tended to be shaped in long strips.

In the days of the scratch-plow, fields were distributed generally in units capable of supporting a single family. Subsistence farming was the presupposition. But no peasant owned eight oxen: to use the new and more efficient plow, peasants pooled their oxen to form large plow-teams, originally received (it would appear) plowed strips in proportion to their contribution. Thus, distribution of land was based no longer on the needs of a family but, rather, on the capacity of a power machine to till the earth. Man's relation to the soil was profoundly changed. Formerly man had been part of nature; now he was the exploiter of nature.

Nowhere else in the world did farmers develop any analogous agricultural implement. It is coincidence that modern technology, with its ruthlessness toward nature, has so largely been produced by descendants of these peasants of northern Europe?

This same exploitative attitude appears slightly before A.D. 830 in Western illustrated calendars. In older calendars the months were shown as passive personifications. The new Frankish calendars, which set the style for the Middle Ages, are very different: they show men coercing the world around them—plowing, harvesting, chopping trees, butchering pigs. Man and nature are two things, and man is master.

These novelties seem to be in harmony with larger intellectual patterns. What people do about their ecology depends on what they think about themselves in relation to things around them. Human ecology is deeply conditioned by beliefs about our nature and destiny—that is, by religion. To Western eyes this is very evident in, say, India or Ceylon. It is equally true of ourselves and of our medieval ancestors.

The victory of Christianity over paganism was the greatest psychic revolution in the history of our culture. It has become fashionable today to say that, for better or worse, we live in "the post-Christian age." Certainly the forms of our thinking and language have largely ceased to be Christian, but to my eye the substance often remains amazingly akin to that of the past. Our daily habits of action, for example, are dominated by an implicit faith in perpetual progress which was unknown either to Greco-Roman antiquity or to the Orient. It is rooted in, and is indefensible apart from, Judeo-Christian teleology. The fact that Communists share it merely helps to show what can be demonstrated on many other grounds: that Marxism, like Islam, is a Judeo-Christian heresy. We continue today to live, as we have lived for about 1700 years, very largely in a context of Christian axioms.

What did Christianity tell people about their relations with the environment?

While many of the world's mythologies provide stories of creation, Greco-Roman mythology was singularly incoherent in this respect. Like Aristotle, the intellectuals of the ancient West denied that the visible world had had a beginning. Indeed, the idea of a beginning was impossible in the framework of their cyclical notion of time. In sharp contrast, Christianity inherited from Judaism not only a concept of time as nonrepetitive and linear but also a striking story of creation. By gradual stages a loving and all-powerful God had created light and darkness, the heavenly bodies, the earth and all its plants, animals, birds, and fishes. Finally, God had created Adam and, as an afterthought, Eve to keep man from being lonely. Man named all the animals, thus establishing his dominance over them. God planned all of this explicitly for man's benefit and rule: no item in the physical creation had any purpose save to serve man's purposes. And, although man's body is made of clay, he is not simply part of nature: he is made in God's image.

Especially in its Western form, Christianity is the most anthropocentric religion the world has seen. As early as the 2nd century both Tertullian and Saint Irenaeus of Lyons were insisting that when God shaped Adam he was foreshadowing the image of the incarnate Christ, the Second Adam. Man shares, in great measure, God's transcendence of nature. Christianity, in absolute contrast to ancient paganism and Asia's religions (except, perhaps, Zoroastrianism), not only established a dualism of man and nature but also insisted that it is God's will that man exploit nature for his proper ends.

At the level of the common people this worked out in an interesting way. In Antiquity every tree, every spring, every stream, every hill had its own *genius loci*, its guardian spirit. These spirits were accessible to men, but were very unlike men; centaurs, fauns, and mermaids show their ambivalence. Before one cut a tree, mined a mountain, or dammed a brook, it was important to placate the spirit in charge of that particular situation, and to keep it placated. By destroying pagan animism, Christianity made it possible to exploit nature in a mood of indifference to the feelings of natural objects.

It is often said that for animism the Church substituted the cult of saints. True; but the cult of saints is functionally quite different from animism. The saint is not *in* natural objects; he may have special shrines, but his citizenship is in heaven. Moreover, a saint is entirely a man; he can be approached in human terms. In addition to saints, Christianity of course also had angels and demons inherited from Judaism and perhaps, at one remove, from Zoroastrianism. But these were all as mobile as the saints themselves. The spirits *in* natural objects, which formerly had protected nature from man, evaporated. Man's effective monopoly on spirit in this world was confirmed, and the old inhibitions to the exploitation of nature crumbled.

When one speaks in such sweeping terms, a note of caution is in order. Christianity is a complex faith, and its consequences differ in differing contexts. What I have said may well apply to the medieval West, where in fact technology made spectacular advances. But the Greek East, a highly civilized realm of equal Christian devotion, seems to have produced no marked technological innovation after the late 7th century, when Greek fire was invented. The key to the contrast may perhaps be found in a difference in the tonality of piety and thought which students of comparative theology find between the Greek and the Latin Churches. The Greeks believed that sin was intellectual blindness, and that salvation was found in illumination, orthodoxy— that is, clear thinking. The Latins, on the other hand, felt that sin was moral evil, and that salvation was to be found in right conduct. Eastern theology has been intellectualist. Western theology has been voluntarist. The Greek saint contemplates; the Western saint acts. The implications of Christianity for the conquest of nature would emerge more easily in the Western atmosphere.

The Christian dogma of creation, which is found in the first clause of all the Creeds, has another meaning for our comprehension of today's ecologic crisis. By revelation, God had given man the Bible, the Book of Scripture. But since God had made nature,

nature also must reveal the divine mentality. The religious study of nature for the better understanding of God was known as natural theology. In the early Church, and always in the Greek East, nature was conceived primarily as a symbolic system through which God speaks to men: the ant is a sermon to sluggards; rising flames are the symbol of the soul's aspiration. This view of nature was essentially artistic rather than scientific. While Byzantium preserved and copied great numbers of ancient Greek scientific texts, science as we conceive it could scarcely flourish in such an ambience.

However, in the Latin West by the early 13th century natural theology was following a very different bent. It was ceasing to be the decoding of the physical symbols of God's communication with man and was becoming the effort to understand God's mind by discovering how his creation operates. The rainbow was no longer simply a symbol of hope first sent to Noah after the Deluge: Robert Grosseteste, Friar Roger Bacon, and Theodoric of Freiberg produced startlingly sophisticated work on the optics of the rainbow, but they did it as a venture in religious understanding. From the 13th century onward, up to and including Leibnitz and Newton, every major scientist, in effect, explained his motivations in religious terms. Indeed, if Galileo had not been so expert an amateur theologian he would have got into far less trouble: the professionals resented his intrusion. And Newton seems to have regarded himself more as a theologian than as a scientist. It was not until the late 18th century that the hypothesis of God became unnecessary to many scientists.

It is often hard for the historian to judge, when men explain why they are doing what they want to do, whether they are offering real reasons or merely culturally acceptable reasons. The consistency with which scientists during the long formative centuries of Western science said that the task and the reward of the scientist was "to think God's thoughts after him" leads one to believe that this was their real motivation. If so, then modern Western science was cast in a matrix of Christian theology. The dynamism of religious devotion, shaped by the Judeo-Christian dogma of creation, gave it impetus.

AN ALTERNATIVE CHRISTIAN VIEW

We would seem to be headed toward conclusions unpalatable to many Christians. Since both *science* and *technology* are blessed words in our contemporary vocabulary, some may be happy at the notions, first, that, viewed historically, modern science is an extrapolation of natural theology and, second, that modern technology is at least partly to be explained as an Occidental, voluntarist realization of the Christian dogma of man's transcendence of, and rightful mastery over, nature. But, as we now recognize, somewhat over a century ago science and technology—hitherto quite separate activities—joined to give mankind powers which, to judge by many of the ecologic effects, are out of control. If so, Christianity bears a huge burden of guilt.

I personally doubt that disastrous ecologic backlash can be avoided simply by applying to our problems more science and more technology. Our science and technology have grown out of Christian attitudes toward man's relation to nature which are almost universally held not only by Christians and neo-Christians but also by those who fondly regard themselves as post-Christians. Despite Copernicus, all the cosmos rotates around our little globe. Despite Darwin, we are *not*, in our hearts, part of the natural process. We are superior to nature, contemptuous of it, willing to use it for our slightest whim. The newly elected Governor of California, like myself a churchman but less troubled than I, spoke for the Christian tradition when he said (as is alleged), "when you've seen one redwood tree, you've seen them all." To a Christian a tree can be no more than a physical fact. The whole concept of the sacred grove is alien to Christianity and to the ethos of the West. For nearly 2 millennia Christian missionaries have been chopping down sacred groves, which are idolatrous because they assume spirit in nature.

What we do about ecology depends on our ideas of the man-nature relationship. More science and more technology are not going to get us out of the present ecologic crisis until we find a new religion, or rethink our old one. The beatniks, who are the basic revolutionaries of our time, show a sound instinct in their affinity for Zen Buddhism, which conceives of the man-nature relationship as very nearly the mirror image of the Christian view. Zen, however, is as deeply conditioned by Asian history as Christianity is by the experience of the West, and I am dubious of its viability among us.

Possibly we should ponder the greatest radical in Christian history since Christ: St. Francis of Assisi. The prime miracle of St. Francis is the fact that he did not end at the stake, as many of his left-wing followers did. He was so clearly heretical that a General of the Franciscan Order, St. Bonaventura, a great and perceptive Christian, tried to suppress the early accounts of Franciscanism. The key to an understanding of Francis is his belief in the virtue of humility—not merely for the individual but for man as a species. Francis tried to depose man from his monarchy over creation and set up a democracy of all God's creatures. With him the ant is no longer simply a homily for the lazy, flames a sign of the thrust of the soul toward union with God; now they are Brother Ant and Sister Fire, praising the Creator in their own ways as Brother Man does in his.

Later commentators have said that Francis preached to the birds as a rebuke to men who would not listen. The records do not read so: he urged the little birds to praise God, and in spiritual ecstasy they flapped their wings and chirped rejoicing. Legends of saints, especially the Irish saints, had long told of their dealings with animals but always, I believe, to show their human dominance over creatures. With Francis it is different. The land around Gubbio in the Apennines was being ravaged by a fierce wolf. St. Francis, says the legend, talked to the wolf and persuaded him of the error of his ways. The wolf repented, died in the odor of sanctity, and was buried in consecrated ground.

What Sir Steven Runciman calls "the Franciscan doctrine of the animal soul" was quickly stamped out. Quite possibly it was in part inspired, consciously or unconsciously, by the belief in reincarnation held by the Cathar heretics who at that time teemed in Italy and southern France, and who presumably had got it originally from India. It is significant that at just the same moment, about 1200, traces of metempsychosis are found also in western Judaism, in the Provencal *Cabbala*. But Francis held neither to transmigration of souls nor to pantheism. His view of nature and of man rested on a unique sort of panpsychism of all things animate and inanimate, designed for the glorification of their transcendent Creator, who, in the ultimate gesture of cosmic humility, assumed flesh, lay helpless in a manger, and hung dying on a scaffold.

I am not suggesting that many contemporary Americans who are concerned about our ecologic crisis will be either able or willing to counsel with wolves or exhort birds. However, the present increasing disruption of the global environment is the product of a dynamic technology and science which were originating in the Western medieval world against which St. Francis was rebelling in so original a way. Their growth cannot be understood historically apart from distinctive attitudes toward nature which are deeply grounded in Christian dogma. The fact that most people do not think of these attitudes as Christian is irrelevant. No new set of basic values has been accepted in our society to displace those of Christianity. Hence we shall continue to have a worsening ecologic crisis until we reject the Christian axiom that nature has no reason for existence save to serve man.

The greatest spiritual revolutionary in Western history, St. Francis, proposed what he thought was an alternative Christian view of nature and man's relation to it: he tried to substitute the idea of the equality of all creatures, including man, for the idea of man's limitless rule of creation. He failed. Both our present science and our present technology are so tinctured with orthodox Christian arrogance toward nature that no solution for our ecologic crisis can be expected from them alone. Since the roots of our trouble are so largely religious, the remedy must also be essentially religious, whether we call it that or not. We must rethink and refeel our nature and destiny. The profoundly religious, but heretical, sense of the primitive Franciscans for the spiritual autonomy of all parts of nature may point a direction. I propose Francis as a patron saint for ecologists.

FRANCIS ON POVERTY AND SOLITUDE

Photograph of convent in Mexico by Sonia Marshall.

PART THREE

Francis on Poverty and Solitude

Excerpts From the Rule of Saint Francis (1221)

THE INTRODUCTION

In the name of the Father and of the Son and of the Holy Spirit. Amen.

Brother Francis requests Pope Innocent III to approve this rule for our brothers both now and for the future. In turn, Brother Francis promises obedience to the pope, just as the brothers are to obey Francis and his successors.

I. OUR BROTHERS ARE TO LIVE IN OBEDIENCE AND CHASTITY, POSSESSING NOTHING OF THEIR OWN

The whole idea of the life of the brothers is to follow the example of Christ by a life of obedience, chastity, and freedom from all material possession. Here is our rule:

"If you wish to be perfect, go, sell all that you have, give it to the poor, and you will have a treasure in heaven. Then, come and follow me!

"If anyone wishes to follow me, let him deny himself, take up his cross, and come follow me.

Selected, edited, and translated from the Latin by the editor.

"If anyone wishes to follow me and does not hate his father, mother, wife, children, brothers, and sisters—even his own life— he cannot be my disciple.

"Everyone who leaves father or mother or brothers and sisters or wife and children or house and property for love of me will get back a hundredfold and will inherit eternal life."

II. How New Brothers Should Be Received and Clothed

Anyone inspired by God to follow our way of life should be welcomed by the brothers. If he seems to be serious about joining us, the brothers should take him right away to one of the superiors without inquiring into his background. The superior, in turn, should make him feel welcome and give him encouragement while fully explaining our way of life. If he decides to stay, then he should quickly sell all his possessions and give everything away to the poor. The brothers and superiors should stay out of all of this. They are absolutely forbidden to take any of his money either directly or through a third party. If the brothers are really needy, then they can accept something that is absolutely necessary for them (just like any poor person), but they are forbidden ever to take money.

When the person has settled his affairs and returns, the superior will give him clothing sufficient for his year of trial: two habits without a hood, a belt, some underclothes, and a waist-length cape. If he passes the year of trial, he can make his promise of obedience. After he has made this promise, he cannot move to a different order or abandon his present one, since papal regulation forbids this, following the Gospel admonition that "no one who puts his hand to the plow and then looks back is worthy of the kingdom of God."

If anyone comes to the brotherhood who cannot sell his possessions because of some complication, encourage him just to abandon these things. If he is a man of good will, that is more than enough. Nobody who is in the bad graces of the church should be admitted.

The brothers who have already promised obedience may have a habit with a hood, another without one if they need it, a belt, and some underclothing. Everyone should wear castoffs patched with sacking and other rags with the words of the Lord as an encouragement for them: "Those who dress in precious robes and seek delights and clothe themselves in soft garments are found in the palaces of kings."

The brothers should continue to do good even if they are called hypocrites; they should be willing to forgo the elegant styles of this world for the robe of glory that they will have in heaven.

VII. On Earning A Living

Brothers, no matter who they might be, should avoid administrative positions such as chancellors or managers of large households. No job that they do take should ever be a source of scandal. They should seek the most humble jobs so that they are on the lowest rung of the economic ladder. They should be servants rather than masters. They are not to live in the houses where they work.

Any brother who has a skill should exercise it as long as it is decent work that can be done in a godly manner. Remember that the psalmist has said, "You shall eat the fruit of the labor of your hands," and the Apostle adds, "He who does not wish to work, neither shall he eat." Every man may exercise the craft in which he has been trained and expect a just recompense for it as long as he accepts no money. When these skilled brothers are out of work, they should beg just as the other brothers do. Brothers may have the tools and equipment necessary for their work.

Every brother should keep busy, for "always be doing a good work so that the devil always will find you occupied" and "laziness is the enemy of the soul." Hence, the true servant of

God is either doing good or praying.

Brothers who have retired to hermitages or other such places should never think of those spots as their own. They should grant hospitality to anyone who approaches, whether friend or enemy, thief or evildoer. If the brethern are gathered for a meeting, they should be hospitable and cheerful. There should be no hypocritical appearance of poety or asceticism. In short, they should be happy, joyful, and gracious as befitting followers of the Lord.

VIII. ON THE QUESTION OF MONEY

The Lord says to "hold yourself free from every malice and evil desire; be on guard against the desires of this world and the cares of this life." Thus, under no condition is a brother to handle money in any form. He is not to use it to buy books or clothes or to accept it as payment for work. To put it bluntly, he should never handle money except to care for a sick brother. The true brother values money no more than a pebble; in fact, if he values money as much as a pebble, he is running a real risk. It would be a terrible thing for those who have chosen the road of abandonment to lose the whole kingdom of heaven for such a trivial thing. Even if money is spotted lying on the ground, let it alone, just as the dust on the ground is let alone, for "vanity, vanity, all is vanity."

If (God forbid!) a brother should hoard up money for any other reason than to help a sick brother, he should be regarded as a robber and a betrayer of our ideals until the moment he repents.

No brother is to accept or to solicit for money. In fact, a brother should never even accompany those who beg for money. He can take any other form of recompense except that one. When there is an urgent necessity, a brother can get money for someone needy like a leper, but he should handle the money even then reluctantly.

IX. COLLECTING ALMS

The brothers who are anxious to follow the humility and poverty of our Lord Jesus Christ should allow themselves only what the Apostle permits: "Having food and something to cover ourselves with, we consider ourselves content." The brothers should consider it a privilege to live with the outcasts of this world: the sick, the weak, the poor lepers, and the beggars on the road. When the need arises, they are to beg without any sense of shame, remembering our Lord, who "set his face like a flint stone" and was not ashamed. Jesus, like Mary and the disciples, was a poor man and a wanderer; he was not above accepting charity. Even when the brothers are rebuffed, they should remember that God will turn their shame into honor. Shame falls on the one who causes it, not the one who must endure it.

Alms are the hereditary right of the poor guaranteed for them by our Lord Jesus Christ. Both the brothers who seek alms and those who give them to the brothers will be amply rewarded. The riches of this world are fleeting, but charity and alms giving are imperishable commodities.

If a brother needs something, he should tell another brother so that there are opportunities to help each other; after all, the brothers should love and sustain each other as a mother does a child. The Lord will point out a way in all these matters.

The Gospel says, "Whoever has something to eat should not despise the one who is without, and the one who is without should not judge the one who has." When there is a genuinely urgent need, the brothers can make use of whatever food Providence provides for them, remembering that the Lord spoke approvingly of David, who ate "the loaves of propitiation that only the priests were allowed to eat."

XIV. How the Brothers are to Travel in this World

Here is how the brothers are to travel:

". . . with neither purse, nor sack, nor bread, nor money, nor staff.

When they stop let them eat and drink what their hosts offer.

Do not put up resistance to offenses.

If one strikes on the right cheek, offer the other.

If one takes away your cloak, offer your mantle.

Give what is asked of you, and if someone takes from you, do not ask for it back."

XV. More on Traveling

No brother who is traveling (and this goes for clerics as well as lay brothers) is to have a horse or accept a ride on one. The only exception to this rule is in case of great urgency or illness.

Selections from The Legend of the Three Companions

. . . Francis went to the bishop of Assisi, who welcomed him openly. The bishop said to him, "Your father is extremely upset and scandalized by your behavior. If you really want to serve God, give him back any money that belongs to him; after all, it could be money that has been acquired unjustly in business, and God does not want you to spend tainted money in the service of the church. Besides, it may mollify your father a bit to get the money back. Have faith in God, my son, and act boldly! Fear nothing, for God will help you, and the church can provide whatever is necessary for you to live."

Francis was encouraged by the words of the bishop and quite willingly put all his money at the bishop's feet, saying, "My Lord, I am willing to give back not only this money but even the clothes off my back." With that he went into a nearby room in the bishop's palace, took off all his clothes, and, on returning, piled them at the feet of the bishop along with the money. Standing there nude, he spoke to his father, the onlookers, and the bishop:

"Everyone listen to me very carefully. Up to this time I called

---

Selected, edited, and translated from the Latin by the editor.

Pietro Bernardone my father. But because I want to serve God alone, I'm returning these clothes and this money so that now I can say, 'Our Father who art in heaven' not 'Pietro Bernardone, my father.' "

As he stood speaking, all those who were present could see that he had been wearing a hair shirt under his expensive clothes. Meanwhile his father, beside himself with rage and grief, gathered up the clothes and money and left. There were those who were quite outraged by his behavior, since he left his son without even clothing, and they likewise felt a great pity for the young man.

The bishop however, intuiting the great spiritual strength of the boy, gathered him in his own arms and covered his nakedness with his own cape.

[Chapter VI]

The blessed Father Francis taught the brothers to seek the word of God and nothing else from books; he commanded them to possess few books, and the ones they did have were to be for the common use of all. Their beds—if they could be called that —were to be little piles of straw covered with poor rags. He often instructed the brothers that they should live in poor huts or cottages made of wood. They were to resolutely avoid building anything in stone. He not only hated any ostentation in the style of the dwellings but likewise disliked useless ornament or attempts at elegance in furnishings. Not did he want any worldly looking implements at table. Everything was to speak of poverty and cry out that man was in pilgrimage and a wanderer through this life.

[Chapter XXIII]

While Saint Francis was preaching in a certain town, a poor man approached his begging for alms. Saint Francis felt very sorry for the man and commented on his sickly frame and general shabbiness. His companion answered, "Brother, it is true that he looks poor, but it could well be a ruse; he could be the richest man in the province."

Saint Francis was enraged to hear this callous remark and said, "Take off your tunic and prostrate nude before that poor man, confess your words, and ask for forgiveness! When you sin against that poor man, you sin against Christ. When a poor man approaches, always remember that he comes in the name of Christ, who assumed our poverty."

[Chapter XXX]

An old and poor woman who had two sons as friars once came to Saint Mary of the Angels to beg alms from Saint Francis. The saint went immediately to Brother Peter of Catania (who was the minister general at the time) and asked if there was anything to give the woman, adding that a mother of a friar was a mother of all the friars. Brother Peter answered, "the only thing in the house is a copy of the New Testament, which we use to read the lessons during the night office." Saint Francis said to him, "Give her the Bible; it will be more pleasing to God that she should have it than that we should read from it." Thus, she got the first New Testament that the brotherhood had owned.

[Chapter LX]

Once a poor man begged an alms from Saint Francis. The saint had nothing at all to give him, so he got a knife and cut off part of his tunic to give to the old man, for he did not want him to go away empty-handed.

[Chapter LXVI]

On Piously Living in a Hermitage

THE TEXT

Those who wish to retire to hermitages to live spiritually should number three or four at most. Two of these should act as mothers and have the care of two or, at least one friar as sons. The former shall live as Martha, while the others shall live as Mary.

Those who follow the example of Mary shall have an enclosed place, and each one should have a hut so that they need not sleep or eat together. Let them recite Compline at sundown and then observe silence until they get up and recite their Hours at Matins, and "let them seek first the kingdom of God and its justice." At the stipulated times let them say Prime and Terce; after Terce they may break their silence in order to go to their mothers to request an alms just as the poor must do. Then let them say Sext, None, and Vespers at the appointed time.

In the enclosure where the brothers stay, everyone else should stay out, and nobody should eat there.

Those brothers who act as mothers should avoid all other

Probably written by the saint in 1218, this is a short rule for the brothers during their time of retreat. Modern visitors to Assisi can still visit the *carceri* ("prisons") where the early Franciscans went for retreat after their preaching journeys. Translated from the Latin by the editor.

persons and, just as their superiors have instructed them, they should keep all others away from those who have been entrusted to their care. The sons should speak to no one except their mothers and the superior if it should happen that he visits to bring God's blessing.

The sons and the mothers should exchange roles when it seems advantageous to do so. Let them then carry out what has been written above.

The Little Testament (1226)

Write that I bless all my brothers who are in our order, and I bless all those who will enter until the end of time. Since I am weak and suffering from my sickness and cannot speak, I will express my will to the brothers in three, short thoughts. In deference to my memory, my will, and my blessing, let them.

> always love each other;
> always love our Lady, Holy Poverty;
> always be faithful to the prelates and
> clerics of Holy Mother the Church.

Saint Francis dictated this short piece to a priest, Benedict of Prato, just a few months before his death. Translated from the Italian by the editor.

Selections from the Fioretti

How Saint Francis Spent An Entire Lent Subsisting on a Half Loaf of Bread

The true servant of Christ, Saint Francis, was in so many ways another Christ given to the world by God for the salvation of souls. God the Father wished to have Saint Francis conformed in many of his activities to those of his Son Jesus Christ, as one clearly sees in the fact that Saint Francis had twelve followers at the beginning, in his stigmata, and in the way he continually fasted during the period of Lent. This latter fact will now be narrated.

One year on carnival day Saint Francis was staying in the house of a friend on the shore of a lake near Perugia. He was inspired by God to spend Lent on an island of that lake. Saint Francis then requested his friend to row him out to that island without anyone knowing about it on the evening of Ash Wednesday. The friend, who loved Saint Francis a great deal, was happy to comply with his wish, and he took him to the island. Saint Francis took only two loaves of bread with him. When they got to the island, Saint

Translated from the Italian by the editor.

111

Francis left his friend, and before the friend left, he begged him to tell nobody where he was. The friend was told to return on Holy Thursday. And so he left the saint.

Saint Francis remained alone. There was no habitation on the island, so Saint Francis went into the woods where a stand of plum trees and saplings had formed a natural lair almost like a small hut. There Saint Francis remained to pray and contemplate the things of heaven. He stayed there throughout Lent and ate only one half of a loaf, for when the friend returned on Holy Thursday, he found one loaf untouched and half of another. It is believed that Saint Francis ate the half loaf out of respect for the Blessed Christ, who fasted forty days and nights without touching earthly food. So on the strength of that half loaf, Saint Francis drove out vainglory from his body, and following the example of Christ, he fasted forty days and nights.

Since Saint Francis sanctified that place by his great abstinence, God worked many miracles there through his merits. Men began to build there and live; afterward a beautiful and strong castle was built and then a convent for the brothers which is now called "the place of the island." Even to this day the men and women of the settlement have a great reverence for the place where Saint Francis spent Lent.

In the praise of Christ. Amen.

[Chapter VII]

How Saint Francis in a Trip to France Lifted Brother Masseo in the Air by His Breath Alone

The great servant and follower of Christ Saint Francis wished always to conform himself perfectly to the example of Christ. Since the Gospel tells us that he sent his disciples two by two to diverse cities and places, so also Saint Francis, following this example, sent twelve of his brothers to preach two by two. To give the brothers a true example of obedience, he started out first, for this was the method of Christ, who first did before he taught.

Having assigned brothers to diverse parts of the world, he set out with Brother Masseo as a companion to go to the province of France. Arriving at a certain town, they set out to beg for bread in the name of God's love, for they were hungry. Saint Francis took one path, and Brother Masseo, a different one. Because Saint Francis was a small man and of unprepossessing appearance, the type that men would spurn when they did not know him, he succeeded in getting only a few scraps and crusts of dry bread. But Brother Masseo, who was good looking and robust in body, came back with large chunks of bread and even an entire loaf.

After they finished begging, they met together outside the town in order to eat. It was a beautiful spot with a pretty well and a large stone where they were able to put out the things that they had received. When Saint Francis saw the large pieces that Brother Masseo had brought, he was very happy and said, "Brother Masseo, we are not even worthy of such delicacies." Since he repeated this a number of times, Brother Masseo remarked, "How can you call this a treasure, since this is such poor food, and we lack all the things that we need to eat? There is neither napkin, knife, cutting board, bowl, table, house, or servant."

Saint Francis responded, "This is what I call a great treasure. There is nothing here from human industry, but everything comes from the providence of God. Look about you. We have bread that is begged, a good stone for a table, and clear water from the well. So I want us to pray to God that this treasure of holy poverty, noble thing that it is, for it has God as provider, will make us love him with all our hearts." When he finished speaking, they ate, said their prayers, and continued on their journey.

Reaching a church, Saint Francis said to his companion, "Let's go in here and pray." Then Saint Francis went by an altar and began to pray. While praying, he received a divine visitation that

so inflamed his soul with the love of holy poverty that it seemed
as if flames full of love were darting out from his glowing face and
his mouth.

And approaching his companion, he said to him, "A—A—A—
Brother Masseo, come to me." He said this three times, and at
the third time Saint Francis, with the power of his breath, lifted
him in the air and thrust him forward nearly a spear's length.

After that event Brother Masseo, who had been stupified by it,
told his friends that when Saint Francis had lifted him by the
power of breath, he had felt the consolation of the Holy Spirit
and a sweetness of soul that he had never before experienced.

After this all happened Saint Francis said, "My dear companion, let's go to the church of Saint Peter and Paul and pray that
they will teach us how to attain the immensurable gift of holy
poverty. That treasure is so valuable and divine that we are not
really worthy to carry it within ourselves. It is a heavenly strength
that crushes underfoot all earthly and transitory things; it
removes every obstacle from the soul that might hold it back from
freely flying to God. This is the virtue that permits the earthly
soul to speak to the angels in heaven. It is the virtue that accompanied Christ on the cross; it was buried with Christ, rose with
him, and went with him to heaven. It permits the souls that love
it easy access to heaven and is the strong guardian of humility and
charity. Let us pray then to the Holy Apostles, who were perfect
lovers of this evangelical pearl, that they obtain this virtue for us
from our Lord Jesus Christ and that through his holy mercy, we
may be worthy to be true lovers and practitioners of that most
precious, lovely, and evangelical virtue, poverty."

While talking in this manner, they finally arrived at Rome and
entered the basilica of Saint Peter's. Saint Francis began to pray
in one corner of the church, and Brother Masseo, in another.
After a long time of praying with copious tears and much devotion, the Holy Apostles Peter and Paul appeared to Saint Francis
with great splendor, and they said to him, "You have prayed and
begged to observe that virtue that Christ and his Holy Apostles

have followed. Our Lord Jesus Christ has sent us to say that your prayer has been heard. Holy poverty has been granted to you and to your true followers. Furthermore we declare that whoever follows your example perfectly will be sure of the blessedness of eternal life, and all these followers will be blessed by God." Having spoken these words, they disappeared, leaving Saint Francis filled with consolation.

Saint Francis then got up from his devotions, went and found his companion, and asked him if God had revealed anything to him. But he said no, nothing. Saint Francis then told him that the Holy Apostles had appeared to him and what they revealed. Full of happiness, they decided to go back to Spoleto and forget about the trip to France.

To the praise of Christ. Amen.

[Chapter XIII]

How Saint Francis Explained a Vision of Brother Leo's

One time Brother Leo was taking care of Saint Francis, who was gravely ill. While he was at his side, Brother Leo, deep in prayer, was wrapped in ecstasy and was carried in spirit to the bank of a wide, turbulent, and deep river. Watching those who wished to ford the river, he saw a large number of brothers weighted down with heavy burdens who tried to cross but who were swept downstream by the rushing of the water and drowned. Some got a third of the way across, some made midstream, and a few almost reached the far bank. All, because of their burdens and the rushing waters, finally gave up and were drowned. Brother Leo, seeing all this, was overcome by his pity for them. While still standing there, he saw other friars in large numbers, without any weight or burden, gleaming, as it were, in their holy poverty; they entered the stream of the river and made the crossing safely. After this vision, Brother Leo returned to his senses.

Saint Francis, aware that Brother Leo had had a vision, called him over and asked what he had seen. After Brother Leo had recounted the vision in complete detail, Saint Francis said to him, "What you have seen is the truth. The great river is the world. The brothers who drown in it are those who do not follow the counsels of the Gospel, especially that of noble poverty. Those who ford the river without difficulty are the brothers who neither seek nor possess any earthly or fleshly thing in this world but with humble food and modest dress are content to follow the naked Christ on the cross. They joyfully and willingly carry the weight and the sweet burden of Christ and of his holy obedience. They, therefore, without any difficulty go from this temporal life to life eternal."

In the praise of Christ. Amen.

[Chapter XXXVI]

How Saint Francis Prayed for a Nobleman, and He Later Became a Friar

Saint Francis, the servant of Christ, one evening arrived at the house of a noted gentleman. The saint was received into the household, along with his companion, with great courtesy and devotion as if they were angels of God. Because of their reception, Saint Francis truly loved that household, for he had been embraced, had his feet washed, dried, and tenderly kissed, a good fire had been laid, and the table was set with good foods. While they ate, the gentleman waited on them with all care. When Saint Francis and his companion had finished their meal, the nobleman said to them, "Father, I offer you all that is mine. Tell me your needs. If you want a habit, cloak, or a hood, please go and buy it, and I will pay the bill. I am quite willing to provide for all your needs, for, by the grace of God, I have been blessed by many material things. For the love of God, I will do what I can for you and for the poor."

Saint Francis was much impressed by the generosity and courtesy of this good man for whom he had a great love. When he left his home, he said to his companion, "This man would be a noteworthy addition to our order. He knows and loves God so well and is so courteous to his neighbor and to the poor. My brother, courtesy is one of the characteristics of God, who provides sun and rain for the just and unjust alike out of a spirit of courtesy. Courtesy is the sister of love. It cancels out hate and nourishes love. Since I have seen such divine grace in this good man, I would like to have him as a brother. So I want to return to him in the hope that God may have touched his heart to inspire him to come with us as a servant of Christ. For this grace we will pray to God to put this idea into his mind and heart and give him the grace to carry it out."

Oh, the miracle of God! Within a short time after Saint Francis prayed, God did put his desire into the heart of the nobleman. Saint Francis said to his companion, "Let us go to the courteous nobleman, my brother, for I have learned from God that he, who was so courteous in temporal things, will now also be generous with himself and join our company."

So off they went, and when they were close to his house, Saint Francis said to his companion, "Wait a bit here for me, because I want to pray so that our trip shall not be in vain. For we hope to gain one from the world, and may it please Christ to grant it to us, so weak and ignoble, by the power of his holy Passion." He then began to pray in a place where he could be seen by the nobleman.

By the grace of God, the nobleman saw Saint Francis praying before Christ in a most devout manner. Christ had appeared to the saint, and the nobleman saw Francis bodily lifted off the ground in ecstasy for a length of time. The nobleman was truly touched by this scene, and he decided to leave the world. He rushed from his palace and in an inspired run hastened to the feet of Saint Francis and knelt before the saint, who was still in prayer. He begged him to be allowed to do penance with him. Saint Francis saw that his prayer had been heard by God. He got up with great joy and happiness of spirit, embraced and kissed the nobleman while devoutly thanking God, who had sent such a worthy knight to join the ranks of his order.

The nobleman then said to Saint Francis, "What do you order me to do, holy father? I am prepared to give everything away to the poor so that I can follow Christ with you penniless if that is your will." And that is what he did. With the advice and help of Saint Francis, he distributed all his patrimony to the poor and entered the order, where he lived a life of penance, sanctity of life, true conversion right to the end of his days, when he went to eternal glory.

In the praise of Christ. Amen.

[Chapter XXXVII]

FRANCIS AND WOMEN

"Sleeping Muse." Artist: Constantin Brancusi. Metropolitan Museum of Art. Alfred Stieglitz Collection, 1949.

PART FOUR

Francis and Women

Selections from the Fioretti

How the Citizens of Assisi Ran to Saint Mary of the Angels to Put Out a Fire

When Saint Francis was in Assisi, he often visited Saint Clare in
order to give her spiritual counsel. She had a great desire to eat
with Saint Francis and had asked him many times, but he never
granted her this consolation. Some of his companions came to
Saint Francis once to talk about the desire of Clare and said to
him, "Father, we do not think that this rigidity is in keeping with
divine love. You do not want to grant such a little thing as a meal
to Sister Clare, a virgin who is so holy and so beloved of God.
It was through your preaching that she abandoned the world and
her riches, and that should be kept in mind. Even if she were to
ask a greater favor, you ought to grant it since she is your spiritual
offspring."

Saint Francis said, "Do you think then that I should grant her
request?"

His friends said, "Yes, father. She is worthy of this grace."

Saint Francis then said, "If it seems good to you, then it seems

Translated from the Italian by the editor.

good to me. It would be better for her to come here to Saint Mary of the Angels, for she has been cloistered so long at Saint Damian's and it would be pleasing to her to see again the place where her hair was cut and where she became a bride of Christ. So, in the name of God, we will eat here."

When the time came Saint Clare left her convent with a companion and accompanied by the brothers of Saint Francis. When she arrived at Saint Mary of the Angels, she devoutly saluted the Virgin Mary at the altar where she had been first veiled and tonsured. Then she found a place to wait until the hour of the meal.

In the meantime Saint Francis prepared a meal and spread it on the ground, as was his custom. When the hour came Saint Francis sat with Saint Clare, his companion sat with hers, and the other brothers humbly ringed themselves around the table. With the first plate Saint Francis began to speak softly and persuasively and wonderfully of God. The grace of God descended on the whole company, and shortly they were all rapt in the contemplation of God.

While they were so rapt with their eyes and hands reaching toward the heavens, the citizens of Assisi and Bettona and the people in the environs of Saint Mary of the Angels saw the church, the land, and the forest around enveloped in fire. The citizens of Assisi ran to the place to put out the blaze, for they were convinced that everything would be lost in a holocaust. When they arrived there, they found nothing burning at all. Entering the place, they found Saint Francis and Saint Clare and all the others rapt in the contemplation of God while seated around a meager meal.

They understood immediately that the fire they saw was divine and not material. They were sure that God had made the fire appear miraculously so as to illustrate the fire of divine love which burned in the hearts of those holy brothers and nuns. They returned home happy and edified in their hearts. After a length of time Saint Francis and Saint Clare came to their senses, and they were so filled with spiritual food that they had no appetite for the meal before them. So that finished the meal, and Saint Clare, well accompanied, returned to Saint Damian's.

When the sisters saw her coming back, they were overjoyed, for they were afraid that Saint Francis may have been ready to send her off to be head of another convent, as he had sent Sister Agnes, the blood sister of Saint Clare, to govern the convent of Monticelli in Florence. Saint Francis had once said to St. Clare, "Be prepared should I need to send you to some other place." And she, as true child of obedience, had said in reply, "Father, I am ready to go wherever you wish to send me." It was for this reason that the sisters were so happy on seeing Saint Clare coming back to them to stay.

In the praise of Christ. Amen.

[Chapter XV]

How Saint Clare, Being Very Ill, Was Taken From Her Cell to Church by the Miraculous Hand of God

One time on Christmas Eve, Sister Clare was very sick and unable to go to the church with the other sisters. When they left for Matins she had to remain in her cell and was disappointed that she could not enjoy the spiritual consolation of celebrating the Nativity of the Lord.

But Jesus Christ, her true spouse, not wishing to abandon her, had her miraculously transported by angels to the church of Saint Francis, where she heard Matins, attended the midnight mass, received Holy Communion. She was then returned to her cell.

When the nuns returned to their home, they went to her and said, "Sister Clare, our mother, what a great joy we have felt on this eve of Christ's Nativity; would that it had pleased God for you also to celebrate this feast with us." Saint Clare answered, "I praise and render thanks to our Lord Jesus Christ, my dear sisters and little daughters, for I was there—perhaps even more so than you—at these solemnities. It was a great consolation for me, because through the intervention of Saint Francis and the grace of our Lord Jesus Christ, I was present bodily at the church of Saint Francis and heard with my own ears the singing and the organ music and received Holy Communion. Therefore, rejoice with me and thank our Lord Jesus Christ for his grace. Amen.

[Chapter XXXV]

How Saint Clare Blessed the Food at Table at the Command of the Pope and, By a Miracle of God, the Sign of the Cross Appeared on Each Loaf

Saint Clare, a devoted follower of the cross of Christ and the noble flower of Saint Francis, was so holy that not only bishops and cardinals but even the pope himself came to see her and listen to her.

One time the pope came to the monastery to hear her discuss heavenly things, and while they were discussing the things of God, Saint Clare set the table and placed bread on it for the pope to bless. When their holy conversation had ended, Clare begged the pope on bended knee to bless the food on the table. The pope answered, "My most beloved sister Clare, I wish to have you bless this bread and make the sign of the cross over it, for you are totally dedicated to the cross of Christ."

Saint Clare answered, "Most holy father, forgive me, but it would be an inexcusable thing for a poor woman like myself to do such a thing in the presence of the vicar of Christ." But the pope answered, "So that nobody can think it is presumption but only out of obedience, I order you under the vow of holy obedience to bless this bread with the sign of the cross."

Unhesitatingly, Saint Clare obeyed as a true child of obedience and blessed the bread. Incredible to say, at the moment she blessed, the loaves appeared to have beautifully incised signs of the cross on them. Part of the bread was eaten, and part of it was preserved. The pope himself, having seen the miracle, took some of the bread with him and then left giving his blessing to Saint Clare.

At that time Sister Ortolana, the mother of Clare, and Sister Agnes, Clare's sister, were also living in that monastery. Along with many other nuns, they all lived a life of exemplary virtue and great holiness. To them Saint Francis sent many sick people, and their prayers and blessings cured them.

To the praise of Christ. Amen.

[Chapter XXIII]

A Selection from the Legend of the Three Companions

While he lay sick in the last days of his life at Saint Mary of the Angels, Francis called some of his brothers to his bedside one day and said, "You all know how devoted the Lady Jacopa di Settesoli has been to me personally and to our entire brotherhood. I believe it would make me feel much better if you would send her news of my condition and ask her to send me a cloth habit that is the color of ashes and some of that dessert that she made for me so often when I was in Rome." He was speaking of a dish which the Romans call *mortarolo;* it is made of almonds, sugar, and suchlike.

This woman, a widow, was a member of one of the most illustrious Roman families. She was of such high spiritual repute and such a devoted follower of the teachings of Saint Francis that her love for Christ made one think of a second Mary Magdalene.

A letter was written according to the saint's directives, and while a brother was looking for someone to carry it to Rome, there was a knock at the door. The Lady Jacopa had already arrived in a great haste to see Saint Francis.

Translated from the Latin by the editor.

One of the brothers immediately recognized her and ran to Saint Francis to tell him that she had come from Rome along with her son and a large retinue. He asked the saint whether she could come up to see him or if he preferred to go down to meet her. He asked the saint's opinion, for women were not allowed to enter the cloister. Saint Francis said, "The rule does not apply to this woman of faith who has come such a great distance."

In tears the Lady Jacopa went right up to see the sick saint. Amazingly enough, even though she had not received the letter, she carried with her some ash-colored cloth and some of the *mortarolo* that he had wanted so much.

She later told the brothers that while she had been praying in Rome, a voice told her to hurry off to see the saint, because his days were numbered. She was told by the voice to bring the cloth, the food, and a large quantity of wax and incense (the wax had also been requested in the letter but not the incense). It seems that she had not only felt constrained to give gifts to the saint on his birthday, for she was also to bring gifts for his death, which was, after all, his true birthday.

She prepared the sweet food for him in the cell, but he could eat very little, since he was so weak and so close to death.

She also made a large number of candles which surrounded his body after his death. From the cloth the brothers made a tunic in which he was buried. He himself ordered a sack to be sewed to put over him as a sign of his humility and as a sign of his love for Lady Poverty.

During that week she visited, the saint gave up his soul to the Lord.

[Chapter LXXVIII]

Francis and Clare

Because of Francis' illness, we could no longer think of going away. Fathei Silvester came daily, and one morning he brought Francis a message from San Damiano's.

"Sister Clara kisses your hand, Brother Francis, and begs you to visit her. She says you still have not been to her convent to bless the sisters; that they still have not had a chance to see you and to hear a comforting word from your lips. They are women after all, and though they are safe in God's bosom, they still have need of comforting. . . . Sister Clara sends the following message through my mouth: 'Bestow upon us the gift of your presence at San Damiano's, Brother Francis, so that we may see you, listen to you, and be comforted.' "

Francis shook his head. "What do you think, Father Silvester? Should I go?"

"Yes, Brother Francis. They're women. Take pity on them."

"Father Silvester, once more I am going to speak by means of parables. Brother Leo, you listen too. Oh, if only all the friars were here to listen!

"One day, the father superior of a monastery expelled one of

From Nikos Kazantzakis, *Saint Francis of Assisi* (New York: Simon & Schuster, 1962), pp. 245–54.

the monks for having touched a woman's hand. 'But she was a devout woman and her hand was pure,' protested the monk. The father superior replied: 'The rain is pure also, and so is the earth, but when they join they become mud. It is the same when a man's hand touches the hand of a woman.' "

"Those are hard words, Brother Francis," said Father Silvester, "hard for women to hear."

"They're even harder for men," I said, fearfully recalling all the young ladies I had seen in my life: all the hands I had desired to touch. Thousands!

"Think of the Blessed Virgin," suggested Father Silvester.

"No one touched her hand, not even Joseph," Francis replied, crossing himself repeatedly. "You seem to have forgotten Eve!"

"Well, in any case, what answer should I give Sister Clara? She'll be standing at the door of San Damiano's waiting for me. What shall I tell her?"

"Tell her I'll come when the road from the Portiuncula to San Damiano's is covered with white flowers."

"In other words, never—is that what you mean?"

"Never and always, Father Silvester, are two words which only God may utter. It's possible that right now, now while we are talking, God has paved the road with white flowers. Brother Leo, go and look!"

Father Silvester shook his head skeptically, but I got up and rushed outside, my heart thumping. I started along the path through the woods. It was still morning, and so cold out that you would have thought the ground covered with snow. My heartbeats seemed to ascend to my throat. I was certain of the miracle: I smelled it in the air. Francis' bloodstained face had beamed when he turned and said to me, "Brother Leo, go and look!"— for in his mind the road had already blossomed.

I ran, reached the highway, and immediately let forth a shout: the entire road—hedges, stones, dirt—was blanketed everywhere with white flowers, as far as the eye could see! Falling to my knees, I gave thanks to the Invisible. Then I pulled up a handful of flowers, rushed back to the hut, and entered, breathing heavily from exertion and joy.

"Brother Francis," I shrieked, "the road is covered with white flowers. Look, I've brought you a handful."

Father Silvester fell at Francis' feet and kissed them. "Forgive me, Brother Francis. I shook my head; I did not have faith."

Taking the flowers, Francis placed them over his bloody eyelids and upon the wounds at his temples. "Father . . . Father . . ." he murmured, kissing the petals again and again and weeping.

"Why are you surprised?" he asked, turning to us. "Everything is a miracle. What is the water we drink, the earth we tread, the night which descends upon us each evening with its stars; what are the sun, the moon? Miracles, all of them! Just look at the humblest leaf of a tree, just look at it in the light—what a miracle! The Crucifixion is painted on one side; you turn the leaf over on the other and what do you see: the Resurrection! It is not a leaf, my brothers, it is our hearts!"

Father Silvester kissed Francis' hand. "Brother Francis, you asked for a sign from God and it came: the Lord strewed the road with flowers. Shall I go tell Sister Clara to expect you?"

"Yes, tell her I am coming. Tell her it is not because I wanted to, but because God commanded me. And bring her these flowers which fell from heaven. When they touched the earth they became all covered with blood."

With these words, he gave Father Silvester the bloodstained flowers which he had been holding in his hand.

After Father Silvester's departure I knelt down to light a fire. I heated water and then washed Francis' face, cleaned his feet and hands, and tidied his hair, using my fingers as a comb. He, his arms spread wide, allowed me to tend to him as though he were a small child. When I had finished I took hold of both his hands and lifted him up. But his knees gave way beneath him; he was unable to stand erect.

"How are we going to go, Brother Francis?" I asked in despair. "Your knees won't support you."

"Forget my knees, Brother Leo, and worry about my soul. That will support me. . . . Start walking!"

Biting his lips, exerting all his strength, he left the hut. We started along the path.

"Brother Leo," he said as soon as we were outdoors, "how many times must I tell you that the soul of man is a divine spark —in other words, that it is all-powerful. But we do not know this, and we squash it under our flesh, under our fat. Ah, if we could only let it go free!"

He hesitated for a moment and then:

"You believe I'm unable to walk, do you? You believe my soul is unable to support my body? Now you shall see!"

He began to stride along the path, his knees firm and unsagging. When we reached the wide road we looked for the flowers, but they had vanished—it was as though they had been a layer of winter hoarfrost melted by the rising sun. Francis crossed himself.

"This is a miracle too," he said. "The flowers came down from heaven, delivered their message, and then returned. They did not want human feet to step on them."

Falling silent, he set out in the direction of San Damiano's, proceeding gingerly along the very edge of the road. Sister Clara, followed by two of the nuns, had already left the convent in order to receive Francis. When she caught sight of him she halted, crossed her arms, and waited with downcast eyes; but as soon as she was able to hear the sound of his footsteps she raised her head and blushed to the roots of her hair.

"God be with you, Sister Clara; God be with you all, my sisters," said Francis in greeting, and he held out his hand to bless them.

"Welcome to our home, Father Francis," Clara replied. "We've been expecting you for thousands of years."

She fell prostrate before him and kissed his feet.

"Do not complain, Sister Clara," answered Francis. "I sent you messages regularly through Father Silvester."

Clara prostrated herself once more, requesting permission to speak.

"Messages do not satisfy us, Father Francis. Words which come from far away are nothing but wind, air—and they scatter. We are women. To be calmed we must see the movement of the lips that are addressing us, we must feel upon our heads the hand that is held over us in benediction. We are women, I tell you. If you refuse to come here to comfort us with your words, Father Francis, we are lost."

The two of them walked ahead, still conversing, while we others followed behind. When Francis reached the convent door he halted, swept away by the sight before him. What a lovely little garden—it was Paradise! How sweet the flowers smelled!

"What did you plant in the courtyard, Sister Clare? I can't see clearly."

"Lilies and roses, Brother Francis. And in the autumn we have violets. That's all."

Francis extended his hand and blessed the yard. "Sister Yard, Sisters Lilies and Roses, I am delighted to be here with you! May it please our gracious Lord that on the Day of Judgment you too shall rise from the earth and enter heaven together with Sister Clara."

He stepped inside. The walls were whitewashed with lime; the statue of the Blessed Virgin showed Our Lady smiling as she clasped her Son tightly to her breast. The sisters prostrated themselves, kissing Francis' feet, and he in turn placed his hand on each of their heads and blessed them. They were all tightly wrapped in white wimples, and when they walked, they resembled doves.

A stool was brought for Francis. Clara knelt on the floor next to him, while the sisters remained standing behind, their arms crossed. For a long time no one spoke. Every eye was fixed upon the saintly visitor. How sweet that silence was, how secure we all felt! I was certain that throngs of angels had come down to San

Damiano's and were now standing unseen in the air, waiting like the rest of us for Francis to speak. He, however, was in no hurry. You could sense from the expression on his face that he was rapt in unspeakable exultation.

"How clean, how fragrant that air was," he said to me later; "how long it's been since I enjoyed the odor of freshly washed clothes, and of trunks which fill the room with the fragrance of mint and laurel the moment you open them!"

"Take pity on us, Father Francis; let us hear your voice," said Sister Clara finally, kissing the hem of his robe.

Francis raised his head with a start and stretched his arms, as though awakening. "I am glad to be here, my sisters. What more do you expect me to say? When I was in the world and used to hold banquets for my friends, I would throw back my head and sing:

> A thousand greetings, my friends,
> Ten thousand greetings to you!
> The valley is covered with flowers,
> The fields with verdure and dew.

My sisters, the same song rises now from my heart: a thousand and ten thousand greetings."

He was extremely moved. I had not seen him so happy for ages. This was the atmosphere he loved: the purity, cleanliness, and ardor which now surrounded him—also those white wimples! He spoke again:

"Listen to me, my sisters, and forgive me if I tell you about a caterpillar that just came again to my mind. This is not a story, it's true—truer than truth itself. . . . Well, once there was a caterpillar which crawled and crawled, until finally in its extreme old age it arrived before the gates of heaven. It knocked and a voice came from within: 'No caterpillars allowed here! You're in much too much of a hurry, it seems to me.'

" 'What shall I do, Lord? Command me,' answered the caterpillar, and it curled up into a ball, it was so afraid.

" 'Suffer some more, struggle some more, transform yourself into a butterfly!'

"The caterpillar returned to earth accordingly, my sisters, and began its journey all over again from the beginning."

"Tell us who this caterpillar is, Father Francis," Clara begged. "We are simple uneducated women. Enlighten us."

"The caterpillar is me, Sister Clara, and you, and also all the sisters listening to me, and every person who crawls upon earth. Good God, what feats this poor wretched caterpillar must accomplish before being transformed into a butterfly! Struggle and more struggle, my sisters, ascent along the uphill road, extreme suffering; and purity, love, poverty, hunger, nakedness, tears—all these are required! Satan has laid his snares everywhere; they are just waiting for us to fall in. If you bend down to smell a flower, my sisters, you will find him there; if you lift a stone he will be hidden beneath and waiting; if you see a blossoming almond tree he will be crouching in the branches, ready to pounce upon you. He is in the water we drink, the bread we eat, the bed on which we lie down to go to sleep: Satan is hidden everywhere, my sisters, everywhere—hidden and waiting. What is he waiting for? For our souls to become momentarily fatigued and drowsy, for the instant when they cease to stand as our every-vigilant sentinels, and thus enable him to leap on us and drag us down into hell. My sisters, you are the ones I am thinking of, the ones I pity —much more than the men; because you are women, and your hearts do not steel themselves easily against the beauties of the world. You look upon them and they please you. Flowers, children, men, earrings, silk garments, stunning plumes: my God, what snares! How many women can possibly escape?

"Morning and evening, my sisters, you pray for all those women on earth who adorn themselves with cosmetics and jewelry, for all those women who laugh. In heaven, the Blessed Virgin echoes your prayer. Don't you hear a deep, divine silence above your heads at night, and in the midst of this silence a sound like the rustling of the leaves of the poplar: the sound of invisible lips praying and beseeching? It is the Virgin Mary, and she is praying for all women everywhere.

"But you must be on your guard, my sisters. Do not say to yourselves: 'We have entered the convent, we have escaped the world and are now promenading in heaven.' This thought is a trap, my sisters, a trap laid by Satan. Listen to what I am going to tell you. We are all one—I swear it to you. If a single woman somewhere at the ends of the earth paints her lips, the shameful color spreads over your lips as well! What is the definition of heaven? Complete happiness. But how can anyone be completely happy when he looks out from heaven and sees his brothers and sisters being punished in hell? How can Paradise exist if the Inferno exists also? That is why I say—and let this sink deep down into your minds, my sisters—that either we shall all be saved, all of us together, or else we shall all be damned. If a person is killed at the other end of the earth, we are killed; if a person is saved, we are saved."

Francis' words made my heart pound with astonishment, for this was the first time I had ever heard him embrace the world with such overabundant love. His heart had blossomed luxuriantly in this feminine air; as he looked at the sisters, his compassion sprouted wings which covered the entire earth.

The nuns had all fallen to their knees. Creeping slowly forward until they encircled Francis, they gazed at him in ecstasy, their faces beaming as though being struck by the sun.

Francis felt their warm exhalation upon him. He parted his lips once more:

"The awareness of your presence around me makes my heart expand, my sisters, makes it desire everyone to enter it—everyone, the wicked as well as the virtuous, so that there may be an end to lamentation and wailing both in this world and the next. O God, a rebellious thought is mounting from my heart to my lips. Permit me to reveal it to these women, for they are my sisters. Their hearts are feminine, full of love and compassion—they will understand. Listen, my sisters: Now, at this moment—

O God, forgive me!—I feel sorry even for Satan. There is no creature more unfortunate, more wretched than he, because once he was with God, but now he has left Him, denied Him, and he roams the air, inconsolable. Why is he inconsolable? Because God allowed him to retain his memory. Recalling the sweetness of Paradise as he does, how can he ever be consoled? We must pray for Satan too, my sisters; we must pray that our gracious Lord will take pity on him, forgive him, permit him to return and take up his place among the archangels.

"Love: that—God bless it!—is woman's destined role. Satan is an ugly bloodthirsty beast, but if he is kissed on the mouth he becomes an archangel once more. That, my sisters, is Perfect Love. In the same way, let Perfect Love kiss Satan so that his original, radiant face may be restored to him.

"Love . . . Love!" Francis cried until his voice was stifled by sobs. Then he lowered his face into his palms and gave himself up to weeping.

Tears began to fall from Clara's eyes as well. Soon she was joined by all the sisters, and lamentations echoed throughout the convent. When Francis heard this, he raised his head, extended his arms, and said in a troubled voice: "I did not intend to make you weep, my sisters. Forgive me. I came to talk to you about heaven, not about hell, and I wanted you to talk to me about heaven also, so that we all could be comforted. Life is oppressive; if Brother Death did not exist to open the door and let us depart —my God! What an unbearable prison this earth would be, what an unbearable prison our bodies would be! But now (what joy, what an ineffable hope—no, not a hope, a certainty), now the soul has crowned itself with lemonflowers and begun to advance over the stones and precipices of the earth, crying, 'O my beloved husband, my beloved husband—Thou, Lord!' "

One of the nuns felt faint. Sister Clara had the window which overlooked the courtyard opened, and the scent of lilies and roses invaded the air. Then, growing bold, she touched Francis' knee and said in a soft voice, "Father Francis, when I look at you I feel that Adam never sinned."

Francis allowed his hand to rest lightly on her white wimple, "And I, when I look at you, Sister Clara," he replied, "feel that Eve never sinned."

For a long time there was silence, a silence overflowing with sweetness and compassion, as though Francis had never stopped speaking. All the sisters, without ceasing their laments, continued to listen to the unspoken words. It seemed to them that Francis was still discoursing about woman's destiny, about love, about the kiss which transforms Satan into an archangel. It was the first time they had felt what an infinitely divine gift it was to be a woman, and also what a responsibility.

Suddenly, in the midst of this hallowed silence we heard violent banging on the street door. It flew open, and in rushed the friars from the Portiuncula. They were quivering with fright.

Clara jumped to her feet. "What's wrong, my brothers? Why did you force our door?"

Juniper wiped the sweat from his brow and replied, "Forgive us, Sister Clara, but while we were at the Portiuncula we saw flames leaping toward the sky. Your convent is on fire!"

"Fire! Fire!" screamed all the brothers. "Fire, Sister Clara!"

But Clara smiled. "You did not see flames, my brothers; it wasn't a fire you saw, it was simply Father Francis talking."

The sun was about to set. Francis rose and said goodbye to Clara and the sisters. Once more he blessed them, placing his hand on the head of each.

"You did a wonderful thing for us, Father Francis," said Clara. "You consoled woman's inconsolable heart. Now what can we do for you?"

"I actually do have something to ask of you, my sister. A very great favor."

"Command us, Father Francis," cried all the nuns.

"I would like you to beg a patch from each poor man you meet, and with the patches you collect, to sew me a robe. This is the favor I ask of you."

Clara kissed his hand. "Why don't you ask me to give you my very life, Father Francis? Next Sunday, God willing, we shall deliver the robe you desire to Father Silvester, and he will bring it to you."

We left, Francis walking in the lead with firm knees while the rest of us followed, conversing jubilantly about the miracle. Behind us, Clara and the sisters stood at the street door of the convent to watch us depart, and many were the tears they were forced to wipe from their eyes.

FRANCIS THE MYSTIC

"Chariot." Artist: Alberto Giacometti. Courtesy of the Museum of Modern Art.

PART FIVE

Francis the Mystic

Francis: The Lover

As he gazes out of the magnificent portrait by Cimabue, sorrow-
ful and silent, standing alone and a little part from the Virgin as
though he dared not draw near to her, a small, dark-skinned man
wearing a brown habit folded loosely, with a low forehead, eyes
like black olives, a long nose, a puckered mouth, and a scrubby
beard, with wrists as thin as chicken bones and no flesh on him,
we are hardly aware that he belongs to the great order of the
Fathers of the Church; and indeed he does not appear among the
lists of the Fathers, and he contended with no theological problems and attained to no scholarship. He laid down the law, but
it was the simplest law of all, exactly the same law that Augustine
announced at the end of *The City of God:* Have mercy on every
living thing; do unto others as ye would be done by; praise God.
That was all, and for Francis, who called himself "ignorant and
an idiot," *ignorans et idiota,* it was enough. The statement, of
course, contained a pardonable exaggeration. What was learning? If learning meant knowing the songs of the peasants and
loving them, Francis was learned: when he sang, with that soft,
eager, heavy voice, the peasants stopped work and ran to listen.

Robert Payne, *The Fathers of the Western Church* (New York: The Viking Press,
1951), pp. 266–78.

141

"What am I?" Francis asked once, and then told of a dream in which he had seen himself as a little black hen. "Look at me well," he laughed. "I am that hen, small of stature and black."

It is right that Francis should be included among the Fathers, for he puts them to shame. He came at the end of the long process of discovery. With him, the wheel has turned full circle: we are back again in the gold-illuminated days of the apostles and of the early catacombs, the days when to be a Christian was to be carefree, before the heretics had arisen and the disputatious theologians had assumed the role of lawgivers. Francis threw learning away and the world sighed with relief, for learning was already weighing heavily in the cloisters, and the librarians, as usual, were wondering whether they would be able to keep count of the books. "What have I to do with books?" Francis said. "O my brethren, all we need to do is pray."

One feels a very real respect for Ambrose; one likes and admires Gregory; it is singularly easy to feel kinship with Augustine; and there is no great difficulty in penetrating the damp cell in Bethelehem to find ourselves watching Jerome, big-boned and long-bearded, scribbling industriously and taking those immense breaths whose length is reflected in his majestic periods. They are giants, fit to be drawn by Michelangelo, but we would not take them down a country road and we would not sing songs to them. But it is dangerously easy to love Francis even to lunacy.

Perhaps it is because he threw the books out of the window with such a clatter and bang that it can be heard down the ages. Almost he detested books. He was never known to read any book except the Bible, and even that he seems not to have read very extensively: a few passages were enough. One day a doctor of divinity approached him and asked for elucidation of the text of Ezekiel: *If thou speakest not to warn the wicked from his wicked ways, his blood will i require at thine hand.* The doctor of divinity explained that he knew some wicked people, and thought it time they should be warned. Francis said he was a fool. The doctor of divinity insisted that he had heard many learned men comment

upon the passage, and the sense of it was clearly that unless you
warned the wicked, all kinds of evils would be visited upon you
by God. "No," said Francis, "I take the sense to be this. The
servant of God should so burn with holiness that he becomes an
example to others. His splendour and the perfume of his name
should be enough to warn the wicked of their iniquities." According to *The Mirror of Perfection,* the doctor of divinity went slowly
on his way, muttering something about Francis's theology being
"like to the flying eagle" while the learning of the theologians
"crawled with its belly on the earth."

The Mirror of Perfection is not an impeccable witness to the truth,
yet "His splendour and the perfume of his name" is the kind of
phrase Francis would use. Jerome would have grappled with the
text, held it to his breast, choked some wayward sense out of it,
and erected upon the small foundations an edifice of theory
demonstrating the perfect necessity of retribution. Francis was
not concerned with retribution. He hardly ever mentions Hell. If
he went there, he would have addressed the sinners as brothers
and sisters, and unable to bear their torments he would have
blown out the flames.

All the Church Fathers had thorns in their flesh, but it was
Francis who received the stigmata. Thomas was obese, Jerome
was tortured by the vision of the pit, Augustine was tortured with
lust, Ambrose and Gregory with pride. Unlike them, Francis felt
no need to suffer remorse for his gay past or to struggle with
demons. As a youth he had a great deal of money and he liked
to wear coloured coats, the left side red and the right side yellow.
He sang love songs as a youth, and he was still singing love songs
when he was old. He even sang a love song when the learned
doctors were drawing a red-hot poker along the whole length of
his face from the chin to the temple in a futile effort to save his
sight; and he blessed the doctors, who went on to cut the nerve
near his eyes, and he prayed very humbly to the red-hot poker.
When Francis was almost screaming with pain, a brother ob-

served that "God is laying His hand more heavily on thee than is right."

"What a simple-minded little fool you are," Francis observed. "If I didn't know you better, I think I would have shunned your company for talking such nonsense. It's God's will that I should suffer, and there's an end to it."

In such simple ways did Francis speak of the problems which occupied the voluminous attention of the Church Fathers. He sang as sweetly and clearly as the cranes which Dante heard as they swept low over the marshes of Ravenna, and he saw no reason to do otherwise even when he was in pain.

As we read of the Church Fathers, we are made aware of immense strains, heroic efforts, terrible responsibilities. The Fathers of the fourth and fifth centuries were shoring up the ruins of Rome with their naked shoulders. They fought prodigiously, with superlative cunning, against the barbarians and the Emperors and all the tribes of wanton and evil people in the world. All is urgency, the smoke of camp-fires, the trumpets on the towers. Slowly, almost imperceptibly, they drew away from life and found themselves devoted to concepts: righteousness, virginity, the hypostasis, the heresies. It was as though in their exhaustion they had come to believe the battle maps had more validity than the soldiers. Francis was inherently incapable of playing with concepts. He must see real people, dance with them, talk with them, play with them, suffer with them. The disputes of the theologians did not concern the humble farmers of Tuscany. He must make them dance and laugh: it is the simplest way: and if he had no fiddle, he would, says Thomas of Celano, "draw a stick across his arm and sing in French the praises of the Lord." Indeed, with his sweetness and gentleness he was more French than Italian, and there must be some truth in the story that his mother was French, for otherwise it is unlikely that he would have been called Francesco when he was born Giovanni.

If Francis was gay, there were yet moments when he could be terrible. The terrifying part of Francis is only hinted at in the records, though it is indisputably there: at such moments the face becomes skull-like, the little puckered mouth becomes a slit, and there is a horror shining behind the eyes. He said once:

Lift up a dead body and place it wherever you wish. You will see that it does not murmur at being moved, does not complain of the place where it is put, does not cry out at being left there. Placed on a high throne, it looks not up but down. Clad in purple, it becomes doubly pale. Well then, here is a truly obedient man, who does not ask why he is moved, does not care where he is put, does not beg to be placed elsewhere. Such a man, set in a place of authority, preserves his accustomed humility, and the more he is honoured, the more unworthy to himself he becomes.

It is, of course, the monastic tradition which was to flower later into the Jesuit retreat, when the candidate during a retreat assumes in himself the postures of the dying and the dead Christ. But there is an unexpected chill in the phrase: "Clad in purple, it looks doubly pale." He said at another time that he never felt comfortable unless he was reviled. Once, when he saw in a dream an empty throne in heaven, he was told that the throne had belonged once to one of the fallen angels but was now reserved for Francis, and when he spoke of this to a saintly friend, he said: "I think I am myself the chief of sinners." Asked why he should think so, he answered: "If any man, howsoever guilty, had received such mercy from Christ as I, I verily think he would have been far more acceptable to God than I." There is a hint of terrible pride here, but it is no more than a hint: the words are too ambiguous to be understood clearly. There was a similar pride in his answer to Ugolino when he was urged to draw up a rule which followed the conventional practices of the past. Francis replied:

God has himself shown me the way of simplicity and humility, both for myself and for those who wish to believe and to follow me. Do not speak to me of the rules of St. Benedict, St. Augustine and St. Bernard, or any other. For me the only rule is the form of life which God in His mercy has shown to me and bestowed on me. *God made known to me that I was to behave with a madness that the world knew nothing of, and that such madness was to be all the learning that we were to have. May God confound your learning and your wisdom.* May He send evil spirits to punish you, and you shall return to your own place, whether you will or no, and curses shall be upon you.

There was some excuse for the outburst. Francis had returned to Assisi to discover that the brothers, assembling together for a chapter of the order, had built a large building for the convenience of the more distinguished members. To Francis the action was a kind of adultery against his Lady Poverty. He climbed on the roof, and in his rage he began to hurl the tiles down on the brothers below; and he would have stripped the roof if the Commune of Assisi had not pointed out that the building, erected within the city, belonged to the Commune. Glowering with rage, Francis came off the roof. Shortly afterwards, sick of distinctions of rank and sick of learning, he wandered off to Egypt and, making his way through the battlelines with astonishing audacity, bearded the Sultan in his den, took a silent part in the bloody battle for Damietta, and then wandered barefoot over Palestine. It was as though in these perilous wanderings he was attempting to remove from himself that *terribiltà*, the explosive prideful wrath which came to so many men of his time.

Francis's fear of learning was real and undisguised, as the chapter at Assisi showed, yet it was strangely modified. The rule of his order did include, when finally composed, much that was similar to the rule of St. Benedict. Curiously, Francis omitted in his speech any reference to the Dominicans, an order founded ten years before his own. The doctor of divinity who questioned the interpretation of a passage of Ezekiel was a Dominican. But it was not so much Dominicans Francis disliked as all those who talked too much and worked too little. Such people he called "Brother Fly." He must have detested flies as much as he detested laziness, for he talked about flies with deliberate malice.

When some of his friars had collected more money than they needed, he said: "So you have got some flies." It was part of his greatness and his newness that he invented words or changed their meaning. "Money" became "flies." It was also called "asses' dung." Such words were not important. What is important is the extraordinary depth and reverberation he gave to the words "brother" and "sister." There is no indication that anybody at any time before had talked of "Brother Wolf" or "Sister Lark", or "our brother the Sun." He was determined that words should possess familiar meanings. He shocked many by calling the Christ-child "Bambino." Contrary to the established rule, he accented the first syllable of "Bethlehem," saying that in this way he could call to mind the bleating of the lamb Jesus. He attempted to create a language of the affections where there was none before; and it was because they spoke in a language which was not affectionate that he half despised the scholars.

One day a novice came to see him to ask whether he could have approval to compile a collection of the Lives of the Saints. It was a subject on which Francis possessed strong views. He saw no reason to grant the request. He said: "Charlemagne and his paladins performed mighty deeds of valour against the infidels and they died in battle, martyrs for Christ's sake. Then came the poets who made epics from their great deeds and received money for reciting them in the streets and courtyards. It is the same with us. The saints accomplished great deeds, and now there are brothers who desire fame in recounting them." There he left the matter. A few days later, the novice returned to Francis and begged that in this case an exception should be made. He pointed out how the examples of the saints would improve the lives of the brothers. "Will they?" asked Francis. "After the legends of the saints you will want prayerbooks, and then you will climb up into a chair like a bishop and say to your brother in God: 'Go, fetch me my prayerbook.' You see—" At this point Francis broke off, scooped up some ashes from the hearth, and placed them on his head. "There's your prayerbook!" he exclaimed. Francis had been in a rage. He grew calmer, and in a quiet voice went on: "It is given to you to know the mystery of God: for others there is book-learning. So many resort to book-learning that he is blessed who is ignorant and a witness for the love of God." For the second time the novice went away, but he returned to the charge some months later. Francis was ashamed of his bursts of anger, and said: "Well, then, do as your confessor says." Then he added quickly and softly, as though he was talking about something else altogether, though in truth he was still talking about the legends of the saints: "He who would join the brotherhood shall possess only the cloak, the girdle and the pair of breeches, and if he really needs them he may add sandals to the list."

The appeal to poverty gave Francis authority for his relentless attack on the scholars. "The letter killeth," he said repeatedly. In the Rule of 1221 he wrote: "The clergy may have only such books as are necessary for their office, and the laymen who can read may be allowed to possess a psalter." Two years later, in another Rule, Francis wrote: "He who does not know his letters need not trouble to learn them." The order was ten years old before any book beside the New Testament was permitted to the monks, and even this they did not keep, but gave to the poor. Yet in this, as in other things, Francis was far from being consistent. In his yough he had read the *Song of Roland,* and the heroic strains of the French epic are echoed in some of his sermons: they formed, as it were, the ground-swell of his heroic life. He was relentlessly opposed to anyone else's reading them. All evil was in them: surely it was enough that men should contemplate the glory of God. And if he was inconsistent in this, he was inconsistent in his attitude toward the habits of scholarship, for though he detested all books, he ordered that his sermons and conversations should be written down for the benefit of those who came after him, and he was especially careful that he should be reported accurately. Almost there was a scholastic in him. Augustine said once, thinking more of the pagan philosophers than of Christian scholars:

"I accuse not words. I accuse the wine of error that drunken doctors pour out for us in these fair goblets." Gregory, too, though he wrote interminably, came at moments to fear those words which so inadequately expressed his visions. The wine of error! For most of the Fathers scholarship was a heady wine which made them drunk with the glory of words. Francis believed it was of greater moment to be drunk with the glory of God, without words, even without the word of God.

But it was not the lives of the saints, the legends, and the scriptures that Francis feared so much as the commentaries. When he lay dying, having composed his Testament, he begged that it should be read without subtle interpretations, for was not the meaning clear? When he spoke of poverty, he meant poverty; and when he spoke of eternal glory he meant simply that. To him it was easy, since he saw with his innocent eye everything bathed in clarity, but it was not so easy for his successors. Words change their meanings. There is a place for commentaries. In the years after his death inevitably the commentaries arose; there were even commentaries on his Testament, the most subtle disquisitions on the meaning of every phrase; it could hardly be helped. Yet the Testament was simple enough, for in it he announced only that the priests should possess a single habit, a girdle, and a pair of breeches; they must work; they must never enter houses as hosts but always as guests; they must never transgress against Holy Poverty; they must salute each other with the word of peace. He wrote:

We loved to live in poor and abandoned churches, and we were ignorant and submissive to all. I worked with my hands and would continue to do so, and it is my desire that all other friars work at some honourable trade. Let those who have none learn one, not for the purpose of receiving the price of toil, but for their god example and to flee idleness. And when they do not give us the price of the work, let us resort to the table of the Lord, begging our bread from door to door. The Lord revealed to me the salutation we ought to give: "God give you peace."

But what exactly was meant by peace? Was it simply the same greeting Francis had heard among the Mohammedans: "*Salaam aleikum?*" Or did it mean, as it seemed to mean, the peace of the first day of creation? Or was it the peace Francis himself possessed in his heart through all his days?

With Francis a complete break is made with the past. The symphony becomes song again. He did not speak in that overrich medieval Latin, which rings like metal and reverberates like echoes and seems to have been fashioned for the usage of Emperors. With Francis grandiloquence vanished. He would talk as ordinary people talk, or not at all. He refused to invent problems. The Church Fathers discoursed at length on the nature of man. Francis answered briefly: "Whatsoever a man is in the face of God, that is he, and no more." Sometimes, too, he spoke in a child's language, with a child's logic and a child's bad temper. When he had received the stigmata, he had no desire to show his wounds, and when one of the brothers saw the wound on his hand and asked him the cause, he answered bluntly enough: "Mind your own business!" At another time a brother observed some bloodstains on his clothes and asked the reason. In answer Francis put a finger to his eye and said: "Why don't you ask me what this is?" But that childishness, that clarity and good-humour were to have unfathomable consequences: one of them was that he became as he lay dying the first Italian to write a great religious poem in the vernacular, and therefore he became the herald of all the songs that came after.

During the last days of his life, shortly before the doctors cauterised his ears and cheeks and temples in the hope of saving his eyesight from the trachoma which was fast eating into his eyes, Francis lived in a small straw hut beside the monastery wall. He was ill and feverish. The rats came through the straw and climbed on him, and though he loved animals, he made an exception of rats, and was terrified. Their creeping kept him from sleep. They rustled in the straw and gathered the few crumbs on his table. He was in delirium. But one morning, to everyone's astonishment, he was found leaning against a tree outside the hut with his cowl drawn over his face. He had never drawn his cowl down like this before, and now he resembled the ancient Romans who veiled their faces when they approached the gods. At such times the Romans spoke with bated breath, haltingly and ponderously; but the brethren who came out into the garden to hear Francis as he spoke beneath the tree were surprised once again by the singular sweetness of his voice. As so many times before, he told a morning parable. He said: "If the Emperor gives to one of his servants an entire Kingdom, ought not that servant to be grateful? If the Emperor gives to one of his servants the entire Empire, should he not be even more grateful? So ought I to be grateful for my sufferings, and give grace to God, for which I am still in the flesh, He has given me the certainty that I shall enter His Kingdom. Therefore, in praise of Him, and for the consolation and edification of the world, I will make a new song of praise for all the creatures of the Lord whom we make use of every day, and without whom we cannot live, though we are not grateful enough to Him for his help, and often offend Him." For a while he was thoughtful, withdrawn in the darkness of his cowl. Then they heard him singing:

> Most high omnipotent good Lord:
> To Thee be the praise, the glory, the honour and all blessing:
> Only to Thee do they belong:
> And no man is worthy to name Thee.

> Praised be my Lord God with all his creatures, especially our brother the Sun,
> Who brings us the day and enlightens us with it:
> Fair is he, and shining with great splendour:
> O Lord, he bears Thy similitude.

> Praised be my Lord for Sister Moon and for the stars:
> For Thou hast formed them clear and beautiful in the heavens.

Praised be my Lord for Brother Wind and for the air and clouds and
calms and all weathers,
By which Thou givest sustenance to all Thy creatures.

Praised be my Lord for Sister Water:
Who is most useful, humble, precious and chaste.
Praised be my Lord for Mother Earth:
Who doth sustain and keep us, and bringeth forth various fruits and
coloured flowers and grass.

Praised be my Lord for Brother Fire,
Through whom Thou givest light in darkness:
And he is bright and pleasant and very mighty and strong.

Praise ye and bless the Lord,
And give thanks unto Him and serve Him with humility.

This is the "song of the creatures" as we know it, but it was not
the end. Other verses were to come later, dedicated to those who
endure in peace the infirmities of the body; finally, there was a
song about death:

Praised be my Lord for those who offer pardon for Thy love's sake,
Who bear infirmity and tribulation:
Blessed are they who shall endure in peace:
For Thou, O most High, shalt give unto them a crown.

Praised be my Lord for Sister Death,
From whom no living man escapeth.
Woe to him who dieth in mortal sin!
Blessed are they who find themselves within Thy most holy will,
For the second death shall do no harm to them.

In these verses nearly all theology was contained. So artless
that they come with the breath, so rude and vigorous that they
might have been sung by a gifted peasant, they spoke directly of
the things which Thomas Aquinas was to speak about at great
length, and with the utmost difficulty. So it was nearly always with
Francis, who reverenced fire, air, earth, and water like the Greeks,
but with a Christian tongue. At times he seems to emerge from

some long-distant past, from a prehistoric age when miracles abounded and a sense of wonder still informed people, a time when the most casual things assumed a profound significance, and men, animals, and trees were brothers. "Sister Rat," he said once in a long agony before his death, "I am tired and would like to sleep," and it was characteristic of him that he should address the rats gently, though horrified by them.

The last letter he wrote was addressed to Lady Giacoma dei Settesoli asking for a piece of grey cloth to patch his clothes and some of the sweet almond cakes they had once eaten together: The homespun and the sweetness were there from the beginning. For the rest, there was song, which is itself no small part of theology, and he was still singing when he died on Saturday, 4 October, 1226.

If Francis was the most wonderful of the saints, it was because he was the simplest, the most human, the most recognizable; and if we call him a Father of the Church, it is because his learning was prodigious: he knew God, and by knowing God he changed the atmosphere of his times. There was a directness about him which came in the end to be a part of the western tradition: he has left his mark on us all, and we can no more escape him than we can escape the knowledge of Jesus. And as though the continuing tradition of the Church was to be maintained even chronologically, there was born in the year before he died another Father of the Church, who was the antithesis of Francis in nearly everything. Between the humble Francis and the imperious Thomas Aquinas the field of the Church is enclosed.

The Letters of Saint Francis

A Letter to All the Faithful

To all Christians, religious, clerical, and lay, men and women, wherever they dwell in the world, Brother Francis, their servant and subject, sends reverent greetings and prays heaven grant them the true peace and love of the Lord.

Since I am the servant of every man, I am held to serve all and to scatter the fragrant words of my Lord. Conscious of the sickly and weak nature of my body, I know that I am unable to seek out each man, so I hope by means of the following letter (which will be my ambassador) to speak to you the words of our Lord Jesus Christ, the Word of the Father, and the revelation of the Holy Spirit. These words are spirit and life.

I. THE INCARNATE WORD OF THE FATHER

The Most High Father announced to the holy and glorious Virgin Mary through his holy archangel Gabriel the descent from Heaven of the worthy, holy, and glorious Word. In the womb of

---

Written probably in 1215. Translated from the Latin by the editor.

the Virgin he took the true flesh of our humanity and fragility. "While he was rich" beyond all things, he freely chose poverty for himself and his Holy Mother.

At the time of his Passion he celebrated the Passover with his disciples, and "he took bread, gave thanks, blessed it, broke it, and said, 'Take and eat; this is my body.' And taking the chalice he said, 'This is the cup of the New Covenant which for you and for many will be shed for the remission of sings.'" After he prayed to the Father: "Father, if it be possible, let this cup pass," and he sweated as if drops of blood were falling on the earth. But he relinquished his will for the will of the Father, saying, "Father, let your will be done; not as I will but as thou." The will of the Father was that his blessed and glorious Son, given by him for us and born among us, should offer himself as a sacrifice, immolating himself as the victim on the altar, not for himself, "through whom all things were created," but for our sins, "leaving us an example so that we might follow in his footsteps." He wills that we all be saved through his merits and that we receive the Lord with pure heart and a clean body. But few there are who wish to receive him and be saved by him, even though his "yoke is sweet and burden light."

II. THOSE WHO DO NOT WISH TO OBSERVE THE COMMANDMENTS OF GOD

Those who do not wish "to taste and see how sweet the Lord is" and who "love the darkness more than the light" by refusing to obey the commandments of God are damned: of them it has been said by the mouth of the prophet, "Cursed are those who fall from your precepts." But how blessed and favored are those who love the Lord and do as the Lord says in the Gospel: "Love the Lord God with all your heart and soul and your neighbor as yourself."

III. The Love of God and His Worship

Let us love God and adore him with purity of heart and mind, because he asks this above all else: "Ture adorers, worship the Father in spirit and truth." Further: "It is necessary that all who adore him adore in the spirit of truth." Let us offer him our praise and prayer day and night, saying, "Our Father who art in heaven," because "you must pray always without ceasing."

IV. The Confession of Our Sins

We must confess our sins to a priest and receive from his hands the Body and Blood of our Lord Jesus Christ, for he who does not eat his flesh and drink his Blood cannot enter the kingdom of heaven. But, eat and drink worthily, for "he who receives unworthily eats and drinks his condemnation, not discerning the body of the Lord." That is, he doesn't distinguish this food from that which is ordinary.

Furthermore, let us perform "fruits worthy of penitence." We should love our neighbors as ourselves, and if one cannot love another as himself, at least let him refrain from doing him evil; in fact, let him try to do the other a good turn.

V. How Those With Positions of Judgment Should Act

Those who have a legitimate right to pass judgment on others should exercise their office with the mercy that they themselves wish to receive from the Lord. "Amen, I say, there will be judgment without mercy for those who show no mercy." Let us then be loving, humble, and charitable with alms, for these things wash the stains of sin from our souls. The men who have lost all by leaving the world but still carry with them charity and the spirit of giving will receive back rewards and compensation from the Lord.

VI. Spiritual and Bodily Fasting

In order to be Catholics, we must fast, avoid sin and vice, and keep free from overindulgence in food and drink. We ought to make visits often to churches and have respect for clerics (not for their sakes, for they may be sinners) because of the dignity that they have in sacrificing, distributing, and receiving from the altar the most holy Body and Blood of our Lord Jesus Christ. Let everyone understand that no one can be saved except in the blood of our Lord Jesus Christ and through his words which the clerics—and they alone by right—preach, explain, and spread abroad.

Let religious especially, since they have left the world, try to do better and "not omit their obligations."

VII. On Loving One's Enemies and Doing Good Toward Them

We must hate our own body with its sin and vice, for the Lord has said in the Gospel all sins and vices "come from the heart," and "we should love our enemies and do good to those who hate us." We must observe the precepts and counsels of our Lord Jesus Christ. We must also deny ourselves and put our body under the yoke of discipline and holy obedience, as everyone has promised the Lord.

VIII. How Those Who Command Should Be Humble

No one who is avowed to obedience is held to obey an illicit or sinful order.

Anyone who has the right to give orders should remember that "the greater should be as the lesser"; he should be a servant to his brothers and deal with them mercifully, as he would wish to be treated if he were in their place. Nor should he rage against a brother who sins but patiently and kindly counsel him and help him.

IX. ON FLEEING CARNAL KNOWLEDGE

We ought not be wise and prudent "according to the flesh," but rather we should be simple, pure, and humble. We should hold our bodies in low esteem for, through our fault, we are wretched, broken, like worms. The Lord himself has said through the mouth of the prophet, "I am a worm and no man, the despised of men and the hatred of the people." Nor should we seek to lord it over others but rather we should be as slaves and "subject to every human creature for the love of God."

All those who live in this way and persevere to the end will have the spirit of the Lord dwelling in them as in a home. They will be sons of the Heavenly Father and the spouse, brother, and mother of our Lord Jesus Christ: we are spouses when we are joined to Jesus Christ with the bond of the Holy Spirit; we are Christ's brothers when we "do the will of the Father who is in heaven"; we are his mothers as we give birth to him when we carry love and pure conscience in our bodies and hearts. We are likewise mothers as we bring forth good works and show him forth to others through our good works and example.

What a beautiful, holy, and great thing it is to have a Father in heaven! How holy, satisfying, and glorious to have a spouse in heaven! How joyful, wonderous, ineffable, sweet, and inexpressibly beautiful to have such a brother who "gave his life for the sheep." For he prayed to the heavenly Father for his brothers in this fashion: "Holy Father, in your name save those whom you have entrusted to me; Father, all those who gave me in this world were yours, and you have given them to me. The words that you have given to me, I have given to them. And they have heard them and truly know that I have come from you, and they believe that you have sent me. I pray for them, not for the world, that you may bless and sanctify them. Through them I sanctify myself, for they have been sanctified in unity as we are in unity. I wish, Father,

that where I am they will be also with me so that they may see
my glory in your kingdom."

X. On the Praise Due to God

Since he has suffered so much for us and has given us so much
now and promises more for the future, "every creature on the
earth and under the sea" and in the depths should render praise,
honor, and blessing to the Lord. He is our strength and virtue;
he alone is good; he is most high, omnipotent and worthy, glorious and alone is holy, worthy of all praise and laud through all
times. Amen.

All those who neither do penance nor receive the Body and
Blood of our Lord and Savior Jesus Christ, but live in vice and
sin and follow their evil desires and whims while serving the
world with their bodies and carnal desires and serve the devil
with their minds and are so beguiled that they do his work—all
those are blind because they do not see the true light which is our
Lord Jesus Christ. These types do not have spiritual wisdom, for
the Son of God is not in them; of them it has been said, "Their
wisdom will be devoured." They see, understand, and do evil,
and so, willingly, they lose their souls. Learn to see, O blind ones,
deceived by your enemies (i.e., the world, the flesh, and the devil)
that for the body it is sweet to sin and bitter to serve God, since
all vice and sin "arise from the heart of man" as the Gospel
testifies.

But they will have nothing good in this world or in the next.
They believe that the possession of the vanity of the world will
be theirs for a long time, but they are wrong. The day and the
hour will come, and they will not know it or even be prepared for
it.

XI. An Impenitent on His Deathbed

Once a man was on his deathbed, and his friends and relatives
came and told him to dispose of his goods. In the meantime his

wife and children, relatives and friends pretended to cry. Seeing
them cry and tricked by an evil thought, he said, "Look, I'm
entrusting my soul, body, and all my possessions into your
hands." What a fool to entrust his soul, body, and goods into
those hands! The prophet was right when he said, "Cursed is the
man who places his trust in men." They, in turn, called the priest.

"Do you wish absolution for all your sins?"

"Certainly I do."

"Are you ready to render satisfaction to all those to whom you
have done evil and restore what you have received by extortion
or shady dealings?"

"Ah, no!"

"Why not?"

"I can't. I've already given everything I have to my relatives
and friends."

And slowly he began to lose consciousness. That poor, miserable man died a bitter death indeed.

We know that every man who dies in mortal sin without
having made amends has his soul ripped from him by the
devil with such pain and anguish that it cannot be described
unless it has been experienced. All the skills, the power, the
wisdom, and the knowledge that "he thought he had is taken
away." And his relatives and friends take away his inheritance
and divide it saying, "Damn him anyway! He could have given
us more had he been more careful in life." And his body is
eaten by worms. So he loses body and soul and is tormented
in the fires of hell forever.

In the name of the Father and of the Son and of the Holy Spirit.
Amen.

To all who read this letter, I, Brother Francis, your little servant, pray and implore you through the love which is God, to
gather these fragrant words of our Lord Jesus Christ with
humility and love, put them into practice, and observe them
perfectly. For those who cannot read, let others read these words
to you often, remember them, and put them into practice, for

they are "spirit and life." Those who do not do this will render
an account on the day of judgment before the tribunal of the
Lord. But those who take them in a good spirit, learn their meaning, and persevere in them until the end will be blessed by the
Father, Son, and Holy Spirit. Amen.

Letter to the Rulers of the People

To all the rulers and leaders, judges and lords of all the earth
and to all the others that this letter may reach:

Brother Francis, your little and unworthy servant, sends greetings and peace!

Look out and see that "the day of death is approaching." I
beseech you with all the reverence that I can muster that with all
the cares and worries of the world that you bear not to forget the
Lord. Do not stray from his counsels, for all who do that will be
damned and will be forgotten. When the day of death comes, all
those things that you thought to possess "will be taken away."
And those who were the wisest and most powerful in this world
will suffer the greater torments in hell.

I strongly urge you, my lords, that you take care and reverently
receive the Body and Blood of our Lord Jesus Christ in his memory.

Be attentive that the Lord be honored by the people that have
been entrusted to you. Every evening the people should praise
God and give thanks to the Lord at a prearranged signal. If you
fail to arrange this, remember that you will render an accounting
to our Lord Jesus Christ on the day of judgment.

Those who hear the words of this letter and observe its precepts will be blessed by God.

This letter is of disputed authenticity. Translated from the Latin by the editor.

Letter to Brother Leo

Brother Leo:
Brother Francis sends you health and peace.

My son, I speak to you now just as a mother would. All the words which we have exchanged in our travels I can sum up in a single word of advice; in this way it will not be necessary for you to search me out for further advice. Here is my advice: Whatever seems right for you to do to better serve the Lord and to follow in his footsteps and in his poverty, do it with God's blessing and my approval.

But if it seems necessary for your soul or your consolation to come and see me, and you want to come, then come. Do, I beg you, come.

One of the few writings of the saint preserved in autograph, scholars dispute its date of composition. Translated from the Latin by the editor.

Selections from the Fioretti

The Perfect Joy of Saint Francis

One intensely cold winter day Saint Francis and Brother Leo were journeying from Perugia to Saint Mary of the Angels. Brother Leo was a bit ahead, and Saint Francis called out to him, "Brother Leo, grant that God will help the brothers in every part of the world always to be a good example of holiness and edification. But note and mark it down that perfect joy is not found in that word."

Going a bit further, Saint Francis spoke a second time, "Brother Leo, if the brothers give sight to the blind, heal the cripples, drive out demons, make the deaf hear and the dumb speak and, even though it is a magnificent thing, raise the dead, still write that this is not perfect joy."

Still further on Saint Francis cried out, "Brother Leo, if a brother knew all languages and sciences, was an expert in the Scriptures, could prophesy and foretell not only the future but also the secrets of the mind and soul, still you must write down that this is not perfect joy."

Translated from the Italian by the editor.

After a bit, Saint Francis again turned to his theme and cried out again with a loud voice, "Brother Leo, little lamb of God, if a brother spoke like an angel, knew the paths of the stars, the strengths of plants, the nature of birds, fish, and animals, was privy to all the secret treasures of nature, trees, stones, roots, and water—even then you must note that this is not perfect joy."

Further down the road, Saint Francis again cried out, "Brother Leo, even if a brother could preach in a way that converted all the infidels of the world, nonetheless, this would not be perfect joy."

After Saint Francis had been speaking in this matter for about two miles, Brother Leo, struck with wonder, asked, "Father, I beg you in God's name, tell what perfect joy is."

Saint Francis answered, "When we get to Saint Mary of the Angels drenched to the skin, frozen, besepattered with mud, and half-starved and knock at the door, and the gatekeeper answers it and says, 'who are you?' and we answer 'Two of your brothers,' and he says 'You are not brothers but frauds who go about cheating the poor out of their bread. Get out of here,' and then he slams the door so that we are left to spend the night in hunger and cold, and we endure all these insults and cruelties without murmur or complaint against the gatekeeper, thinking that God permitted him to treat us so—Brother Leo, write down that this is perfect joy.

"If we continue to knock and he comes back out in a rage and sends us away with curses and blows, screaming at us, 'Get out of here, you bums, and go to the public hospice, for there is neither bread nor board for you here,' and we take all that with patience, happiness, and pure love—Brother Leo, mark that down as pefect joy.

"If we, frantic from hunger and cold, knock harder, cry out, and implore him in the name of God to open up and let us in, and he, fed up, says to himself, 'Those types are insistent idlers and need a lesson more worthy of their nature' and comes out with a knotted club and grabs us by the hood and hurls us in the snow and clubs us without mercy, and we endure all this patiently and with happiness while thinking of the sufferings of the loving Christ and how we should imitate him—that, Brother Leo, you should write down as perfect joy.

"Brother Leo, let me add a conclusion to all this. Beyond all the gifts and graces of the Holy Spirit that Christ grants to his friends is the gift to endure pain, injury, hatred, and disappointment for the love of him and thus to conquer oneself. We should not glory in any of the gifts that God has given us, for they come from God and not from us, for the Apostle says, 'What have you that you did not receive? If then you received it, why do you boast as if it were not a gift?' But in the cross of tribulation and in affliction we can glory, for they are ours. Thus the Apostle again says, 'In the cross of our Lord Jesus Christ, I glory.' "

To whom be glory and honor forever. Amen.

[Chapter VIII]

How Christ Appeared to Saint Francis and His Companions

In the very first days of the order, when Saint Francis was together with some of his companions in order to speak of Christ, he ordered one of the brethren to speak of God as the spirit led him to speak. The brother quickly obeyed and spoke of God in the most marvelous manner until Saint Francis ordered him to be quiet. Then he ordered another brother to speak. This brother also spoke of God in a most refined manner until Saint Francis ordered him to be quiet and give way to a third so that he might speak. That brother also spoke of God with such conviction that Saint Francis was convinced that he, like the other two, spoke under the inspiration of the Holy Spirit.

That all spoke with the inspiration of the Spirit was soon underscored by a clear sign. For in the midst of them appeared the

Blessed Christ in the form of a beautiful young man. He blessed
them with such a sense of ineffable sweetness they they were rapt
outside of themselves and acted as dead men, so oblivious were
they of the world around them. When they returned to their
senses, Saint Francis said, "My beloved brothers, bless God and
thank him, for he has willed to show forth the treasures of Divine
Wisdom through the mouths of simple men. God has opened the
mouths of the mute and made the simple speak as the wisest of
men."

To his everlasting praise. Amen.

[Chapter XIV]

How a Young Boy Fainted On Seeing Saint Francis Speak With Christ

A very pure and innocent young boy was once received into the
order while Saint Francis was still alive. The place where the
brothers was staying was very small, and so the brothers had to
sleep on the ground. Saint Francis came to this place once and,
in the evening, after night prayers, he went outside to sleep. He
was thus able to get up in the middle of the night and pray while
the other brothers slept, for this was his custom.

This young boy decided to spy on Saint Francis at night, for
he wanted to know about his sanctity, and he was very curious to
know what Saint Francis did when he rose at night while the
others slept. So that sleep would not rob him of the chance, he
chose a place at the side of the saint and tied his cord to that of
Saint Francis so as to know when he got up. Saint Francis knew
nothing of this.

During the night while the brothers were asleep, Saint Francis
woke up and, discovering the tied cord, unloosened it, and got
up quietly without waking the boy. Saint Francis then went off
quietly to go to a hidden spot where he was accustomed to pray.

After a bit the boy woke up and found the loosened cord and the saint gone. He got up and started looking for him. Finding the door open, he figured that Saint Francis had gone into the woods. Getting near the place where Saint Francis was praying, he began to hear a number of voices. Trying to see the place where he was hearing the voices, he saw Saint Francis bathed in light, and about him were Christ, the Virgin Mary, Saints John the Evangelist and John the Baptist, together with a whole host of angels, all of whom were speaking to the saint. When the young boy saw this, he fell into a dead faint.

When the mysterious apparition had ended, Saint Francis was returning home, when he found the boy at his feet in a dead faint. With great tenderness he picked him up and carried him to his bed as a good shepherd does for his sheep. Knowing that he had seen the vision, he ordered the young boy to say nothing during the lifetime of the saint. The young boy grew in the grace of God, was a great admirer of Saint Francis, and gained esteem and eminence in the order. It was only after the death of the saint that he revealed to his brothers what he had seen.

To the praise of Christ. Amen.

[Chapter XVII]

The Admonitions of Saint Francis

I. THE BODY OF CHRIST

Our Lord Jesus said to his disciples, "I am the way, the truth, and the life; no one goes to the Father save through me. If you have known me, you have certainly known the Father; henceforth, you have known him and seen him." Philip said to Him, "Lord, show us the Father, and it is enough." Jesus said to him, "Have I been with you so long, and you have not recognized me? Philip, he who has seen me has seen the Father."

The Father "dwells in inaccessible light," and "God is Spirit," and "No one has seen God." Since God is Spirit, no one can see him if he is not in the Spirit, for "the Spirit vivifies while the flesh is of no value." Nor is the Son, since he is equal to the Father, seen in a different manner than the Father or the Holy Spirit. Thus all those who see our Lord Jesus Christ according to his human nature and fail to see and believe that according to the divine spirit he is the true Son of God are damned. Likewise those who approach the sacrament of the Body of Christ, which is consecrated by the word of the Lord through the ministration of the priest at the altar under the species of bread and wine, and do not perceive or believe according to the Spirit the most holy

---

Composed at various times in the saint's life. Translated from the Latin by the editor.

body and blood of our Lord and Savior Jesus Christ are present are damned. The Most High gives testimony of this: "This is my body and blood of the New Covenant; he who eats my flesh and drinks my blood has eternal life."

Thus those who live with the community of the faithful and who receive the most holy body and blood of the Lord have the Spirit of God; anyone else who does not have this Spirit and presumes to communicate "eats and drinks unto condemnation." Hence we ask, "Sons of men, how long will your hearts be hardened?" Why do you not see the truth and believe in the Son of God? Everyday he humbles himself just as when he came down from a noble throne into the womb of the Virgin; everyday he comes to us in a humble manner; everyday he descends from the bosom of the Father to the altar in the hands of the priest. Just as he appeared to the saints in the flesh, so now he shows himself to us in the consecrated bread; and just as those who saw only his flesh with their carnal eyes but believed that he was God by contemplating him with the eyes of faith, so also we who just see bread and wine with our eyes should firmly believe that his most holy body and blood is living and true. In this manner the Lord is always with the faithful as he himself has promised: "Behold I am with you even to the end of the world."

II. On the Evil of the Will

The Lord said to Adam, "You may eat of the fruit of all the trees of paradise; but do not eat of the fruit of the tree of the knowledge of good and evil."

Adam then was able to eat of every fruit in paradise and be sinless as long as he did not break God's commandment. The one who eats of the fruit of the knowledge of good follows his own will and revels in the good that the Lord says and does in him; but, because of the wiles of the devil and the violation of the commandment, the fruit of good changes into the apple of the knowledge of evil and, of necessity, carries punishment with it.

VII. THE GOOD WORKS THAT SHOULD ACCOMPANY KNOWLEDGE

The Apostle says, "The letter kills, but the Spirit is life." The letter kills those who are greedy only to know words, to be esteemed more intelligent than others, to amass great wealth in order to enrich relatives and friends. The letter kills those religious who do not want to learn the spirit of the Word of God but only its literal meaning and then hand that on to their brothers. Contrariwise, those who live in the Spirit are the ones who desire to know or think they know every word but do not attribute that to themselves but refer all to the Lord, the source of every good.

VIII. ON FLEEING THE SIN OF ENVY

The Apostle says, "No one can say, 'Jesus is Lord' except in the Holy Spirit," and "There is no one who does good, no, not even one." Therefore anyone who envies the good fortune of a brother which has been granted him by the Lord commits the sin of blasphemy, because he envies God himself, who says and does all good things.

IX. ON FRATERNAL LOVE

In the Gospel the Lord teaches, "Love your enemies." Anyone who suffers an offense and is motivated to sorrow because of the sin that stains the soul of the other truly loves his enemy and will show him so by his good works.

X. MORTIFICATION OF THE BODY

There are many who, when they sin or are in error, try to blame an enemy or a neighbor. But that is wrong because everyone has in his power the real enemy, his body, which is the instrument of sin. Therefore blessed is that man who holds that enemy in servitude and wisely guards over it. To be truthful, he who does that need fear no other enemy either visible or invisible.

XI. Nobody Is to Be Scandalized by the Sin of Another

Nothing ought to displease the servant of God except sin. And if, in some manner, another should sin, and the servant of God gets upset or angry so that charity does not move him, he is accumulating for himself a patrimony of guilt. The servant of God who gets neither upset nor angry is living well and sinlessly. And blessed is that one who holds on to nothing for himself but "renders to Caesar that which is Caesar's and to God that which is God's."

XII. The Manner of Discerning the Spirit of the Lord

Here is how one tells if a servant of God has the true spirit: When the Lord does some good work through him, he does not swell with pride, knowing its weakness, but regards himself as nothing and below every other man.

XIII. Patience

No one can know how much patience and humility a servant of God has until things start to go wrong. When the moment comes that those who should be in agreement with him are contrary, the patience and humility he has at that moment is what he possesses and no more.

XIV. Poverty of the Spirit

"Blessed are the poor in spirit for theirs is the kingdom." There are many who pray, practice diverse devotions, penances, and bodily discipline but who, at the first word spoken against them or the first things done against them, are upset and scandalized. These are not poor in spirit, for those who are truly poor in spirit hate themselves and love those who slap them on the cheek.

XV. Peacemakers

"Blessed are the peacemakers, for they shall be called children of God." The true peacemakers are those who for the love of God in the midst of every adversity in this world conserve peace in their soul and body.

XVI. Purity of Heart

"Blessed are the pure of heart, for they shall see God." The pure of heart are those who despise the goods of this world and seek the rewards of heaven. They never cease adoring and looking on the living and true Lord God with purity of heart and spirit.

XVII. The Humble Servant of God

Blessed is that servant who is not prouder of the good that God does or says through him than of the good that is done or said by another. That man is a sinner who wishes to take more from his neighbor than God has seen fit to give him.

XVIII. Compassion for One's Neighbor

Blessed is the man who strengthens a neighbor in his weakness to the measure that he would like to be strengthened were he in similar circumstances.

XIX. The Good and Evil Servant

Blessed is that servant who renders every good thing to the Lord God; he who saves something for himself hides the money of his master, and that "which he thought he had will be taken from him."

XX. The Good and Humble Religious

Blessed be that servant who does not think himself the better either when men exalt and praise or when they think him vile, of little worth, or of no value. What a man is worth before God is his worth and no more. Woe to that religious who when he finds himself elected to a rank above the others does not willingly give it up of his own will. Rather blessed is that servant who when given a high position still considers himself at the feet of all others.

XXI. The Good Religious and the Vain One

Blessed be that religious who finds no other joy or happiness except in holy thoughts and in the works of God. With these he leads men to love God in joy and happiness. Woe to that religious who so loves useless and vain words that he forces men to idle jokes.

XXII. The Talkative and Vain Religious

Blessed is that servant who does not speak for the hope of reward, does not show what is thought of him, and is not "quick to speak" but wisely judges what he is to say and how to answer. Woe to that religious who cannot keep hidden the good things the Lord has shown him, who feels compelled to exhibit them before others in the desire that in such manifestations he may receive a reward; in one way he has received a reward, and the audience has garnered little or no gain.

XXIII. On True Correction

Blessed be that servant who accepts correction, accusation, and redirection from another as if it were coming from himself. Blessed be that servant who, when corrected, accepts it with grace and then respectfully obeys while humbly acknowledging his fault and willingly mending his ways. Blessed is that servant who is not quick to justify himself but who humbly accepts the shame and correction for a sin that perhaps he did not even commit.

XXIV. TRUE HUMILITY

Blessed is that man who acts as humbly among his inferiors as he does around his superiors. Blessed is that servant who stands willingly under the rod of correction. "He is a faithful and prudent servant." He is the one who is not slow to punish himself interiorly and then gets immediately to confession and does penance every time he sins.

XXV. TRUE LOVE

Blessed is that brother who equally loves a sick brother who can render him no service and the healthy one who can reward him. Blessed is that brother who loves a brother when he is far away in the same way as when he is present; blessed is he who speaks the same way when a brother is away and when he is in his presence.

XXVI. THE SERVANTS OF GOD MUST HONOR THE CLERGY

Blessed are those servants who honor the clerics who follow the precepts of the Holy Roman Church. Woe to those who despise them; for, if they are sinners, no one has the right to judge them, because it is the Lord alone who may judge. Since their ministry is far superior to any other thing, in that they function near the most holy Body and Blood of our Lord Jesus Christ and receive it and administer it to others, so when one sins against them, it is a graver sin than sinning against anyone else.

XXVII. THE VIRTUES THAT DRIVE OUT VICE

Where there is love and wisdom, there is neither fear nor ignorance. Where there is patience and humility, there is neither anger nor turbulence. Where there is joyful poverty, there is neither greed nor envy. Where there is peace and meditation, there is neither care nor distraction. Where the fear of God guards the entrance way, there can be no enemy who can find entry. Where there is mercy and judgment, there can be neither prodigality nor hardness of heart.

XXVIII. The Advantage of Hiding Good So It Is Not Lost

Blessed is that servant who "lays up a treasure in heaven" of the goods that the Lord has given him and has no desire to flaunt them before men in the hope of a reward, for the Most High will make manifest his works according to his pleasure. Blessed is that servant who "holds fast in his heart" the secrets of the Lord.

St. Francis and the Stigmata

During the summer of 1224 Francis' health seems to have im-
proved, and in August he left Rieti. The goal of this journey was
the mountain La Verna in Casentino, which had been given to
him by Orlando dei Cattani in 1213; he wished along with the
most faithful Brothers—Leo, Angelo, Masseo, Silvestro, Il-
luminato—to celebrate the Assumption of the Blessed Virgin
(August 15) and then to prepare himself by a forty days' fast for
the feast of St. Michael (September 29). In common with the rest
of the people of the Middle Ages, Francis nourished a special
devotion to this Archangel, *signifer sanctus Michaelis,* the standard-
bearer of the Heavenly Host, and the one who with his trumpet
was to wake the dead in their graves on the Last Day.

Immediately after having received the Alverna hill as a gift,
Francis had sent a couple of Brothers there to take possession of
it. With the help of the Duke Orlando's people the Brothers had
established themselves upon a plateau high up on the cliff, and
had built some huts of clay and interwoven branches, as Francis
liked it; next the Duke Orlando built a little church which received the same name as the Portiuncula chapel, namely, Santa

From Johannes Jörgensen, *Saint Francis of Assisi* (New York: Doubleday Image
Book, 1955), pp. 240–48.

Maria degli Angeli, "Our Lady of the Angels."

During the trip to La Verna, Francis' strength again failed him, and the Brothers went into a farmyard to borrow an ass for their master. When the peasant heard who it was that wanted to use the beast, he came out himself. "Art thou the Brother Francia there is so much said about?" he asked. Receiving an affirmative answer, he added, "Then take care that thou art as good in reality as they say, for there are many who have confidence in thee!" Stirred to his innermost depths, Francis cast himself down and kissed the peasant's feet in thanks for his reminder. May it not have been the same peasant who himself undertook to guide Francis and the Brothers to La Verna? Whoever it was he was seized by an overwhelming thirst in the burning summer heat, and during the long hard ascent from the river Corsalone to the convent. When he complained of his thirst to Francis, the latter kneeled down with him in prayer, and a moment after he was able to lead the peasant to a spring.

"But as now Francis and his Brethren climbed the mountain, and rested a little at the foot of an oak"—the *Fioretti* tell us— "there was at once a flock of the birds of heaven in the place, and greeted them with cheerful song and fluttering of their wings. And some rested on Francis' head, and others on his shoulders, and again others on his knees and hands. But when Francis saw this wonder, he said: 'I believe, dearest Brothers, that it is the pleasure of our Lord Jesus Christ that we establish a residence on this lonely mountain, where our sisters the birds rejoice so much over our coming.'

"But when the Count Orlando heard that Brother Francis and his Friars were going to build on Mount Alverna, he was highly pleased over it, and the next day he went there with many from his castle, and they came and brought bread and wine and other things with them, to Francis and his Friars. And as he approached the place he found them praying, and he went up and greeted them. Then Francis arose and received Lord Orlando and his followers with great love and joy, and they sat down to speak together. And after they had spoken together, and Brother Francis had thanked Count Orlando for the mountain he had given him, and had preached a little, the evening fell. And Lord Orlando took Francis and his Brethren aside and said to them: 'My dearest Brothers, it is not my intention that you shall suffer from want on this wild mountain, and therefore I say to you once for all, that if you are in need of anything you shall only send a messenger to me after it, and if you do not do so I will be very angry about it.' And after he had said this he withdrew with his followers to his castle.

"Francis then made the Friars sit down and determine how they were to live, and he especially impressed upon them the keeping of holy poverty in their hearts, and said to them: 'Do not pay so much attention to Lord Orlando's friendly offering as to break the troth you have promised our Lady, the holy Poverty!' And after many beautiful and pious words about this thing, he concluded, saying: 'This is the way of life I lay upon you and myself. For as I see that my death approaches, I wish to be alone with God and lament my sins. And Brother Leo can bring me a little bread and a little water, as seems fit to him, but if anyone comes, answer for me, and let no one come to me!' And when he had said these words, he gave them his blessing and went to his hut, which was under a great beech tree, and the Friars remained in their huts."

There are still shown by La Verna the places where St. Francis stopped—the great overhanging stone, Sasso or Masso spico, under which he used to pray, the dark damp cave where he had his hard bed on a projecting shelf, Brother Leo's grotto high up on the mountainside, where Francis many a morning in the early hours attended his friend's mass and prayed to the body and blood of our Lord in the white host and golden chalice, lifted on high in Brother Leo's hand as the only comfort for poor pilgrims in this vale of tears.

For again Francis seems to have become disquieted, troubled, and bowed down with thoughts of the future. How was it all going to end? They had taken his Brothers, his sons, from him, and whither were they taking them now? They were going there where Francis did not wish them to go, and he had to look on without power. . . .

In vain did Francis issue his Ideal Image of what a perfect Friar Minor, a perfect Provincial Minister, a perfect General of the Order, should be—he knew well that the facts were widely different. Brother Elias and others of his mind were not, as Francis would have it, satisfied with "a book and an ink-horn and one pen and a signet"—they collected books and studied church law, and it was only waste of time to exhort them to act towards their Brothers in the spirit not in the letter of the law. Again and again might Francis sigh to God: "Lord, I commit to thee the family thou hast given me—I cannot lead them any longer myself!" But again and again the beautiful dream would return, that all was as in the old days, when nothing stood between him and his dear children, and they were united in harmony again and were to be separated no more.

One day Francis awaked out of this his constant dream, and realized anew the truth, and had recourse to a method he had used before, to lift the edge of the veil that hides the future. He ordered Brother Leo to take the Book of Gospels and in honor of the Holy Trinity to open it in three places. Leo did as his master desired, and all three times it opened at the Passion of Christ. Then Francis understood that there was nothing for him but to suffer to the end, and that his days of good fortune were gone forever. And he resigned himself to God's will.

In the night which followed, Francis could not sleep. In vain did he turn on his hard bed—in vain did he listen for the call of the Friars of La Verna, announcing the hour for saying matins. "All will be as it should be in heaven," Francis said to comfort himself; "there, at least, there is eternal peace and happiness!" And with these thoughts he fell asleep.

Then it seemed to him that an angel stood by his bed with violin and bow in hand. "Francis," said the shining denizen of heaven, "I will play for thee as we play before the throne of God in heaven." And the angel placed the violin to his chin and drew the bow across the strings a single time only. Then Brother Francis was filled with so great a joy, and his soul was filled with such living sweetness, that it was as if he had a body no longer, and knew of no secret sorrow. "And if the angel had drawn the bow down across the strings again," thus Francis told his Brothers the next morning—"then would my soul have left my body from uncontrollable happiness."

After the Feast of the Assumption, Francis withdrew from the Brothers into still greater solitude. The place he had selected for himself was on the far side of a deep ravine, and to cross over to it, a felled tree-trunk had to be used as a bridge over the abyss. Here Francis installed himself in a hut, and had made the arrangements with Brother Leo that he should visit him twice in the twenty-four hours, once by day to bring bread and water, once by night at matins. As Leo stepped upon the bridge he was to say aloud the words with which the recitation of the Breviary begins —the verse of the psalm, "O Lord, thou wilt open my lips" (Domine, labia mea aperies). If Francis from the other side gave the proper response: "And my mouth shall declare Thy praise" (Et os meum annuntiabit laudem tuam), then Leo was to go across the bridge and say the matins with Francis. But if he got no answer he was to go quietly home again. "But Francis said this because he was sometimes in such a state of rapture that he could not speak for a whole day, he was so occupied with God," says the Fioretti.

For a while Brother Leo carried out his master's commands correctly. Then there came a night when he stood on the usual place by the bridge and said the usual words. But Francis did not answer.

Now it was a moonlit night—clear with the coolness of autumn, like many September nights in the Apennines. The country lay clear and silent and lonely, and the moonlight on the beech trees looked like snow. The moon shone into the empty hut, and after a brief delay Leo crossed the bridge.

He carefully crept through the trees—there was no trace of Francis to be seen. At last he heard a murmuring as of one who prayed, and by following the noise he discovered Francis. With arms spread out in the form of a cross and his face turned to heaven, he lay prostrate, and prayed aloud. Leo stopped, stood motionless in the shadow of a tree, and now could hear the words of the master's prayer. In the clear, almost frosty night air they reached him one by one.

"O my dearest Lord and God," said Francis, invoking heaven, "what art thou, and what indeed am I, Thy little, useless worm of a servant?"

This he repeated over and over again, until Brother Leo in moving trod upon a twig which snapped. At this noise Francis ceased praying at once and stood up. "In the name of Jesus," he called out, "stay still, whoever thou art, and do not move from the place!" And he approached Brother Leo.

But Brother Leo said afterwards to the other Brothers, that in this moment he was so frightened that if the earth had opened he would have gladly hidden himself in its depths. For he was afraid that Francis, in punishment for his disobedience, would no longer have him with him. And his love of Francis was so great that it seemed to him that he could not live without him.

But Francis came close to the tree and said, "Who art thou?" And trembling all over, Brother Leo answered, "It is I—Leo!" But Francis said to him: "God's little lamb, why hast thou come hither? Have I not told thee that thou must not spy upon me! In the name of holy obedience, tell me if thou hast perceived anything!" But he answered:

"Father, I heard thee speak and say and with much devotion, pray: 'My dearest Lord and God, what art thou, and what am I, thy little, useless worm of a servant?' " And Brother Leo cast himself on his knees and said with great reverence, "Father, I beg thee, that thou explainest to me the words I heard!"

"O little lamb of Jesus Christ," said he, "O my own brother

Leo! In that prayer which thou didst hear, two lights were mani-
fested to me: one light in which I knew the Creator, and one in
which I knew myself. When I said, 'What art thou, my Lord and
God, and what am I?' then I was in the light of contemplation,
in which I saw the infinite depth of the Divine Godhead and my
own wretched abyss of misery. Therefore I said: 'What art thou,
Lord, the Highest, the Wise, the All-good, the All-merciful, that
Thou troublest Thyself about me who am the most miserable
worm of all, a little, abhorrent and despicable creation!' These,
then, were the words thou hearest, little lamb of God! But watch
thyself, that thou spiest on me no more, and go back to thy cell
with God's blessing!"

The days and nights went by—soon the feast of the Exaltation
of the Holy Cross (September 14) would be at hand, the feast in
honor of the winning in the year 629 by the Emperor Heraclius
of the True Cross which the Persian King Cosroes fourteen years
before had taken away with him as conqueror from Jerusalem.

The Cross and the Crucified One had always been an object of
the deepest feeling on Francis' part.

It was the voice of the Cross that in San Damiano's lonely
church in 1207 had converted him from the world to follow
Christ in naked poverty. "From that hour," says the Three Brothers' Legend, "his heart was so sore and melted with the memory
of Christ's sufferings, that all his life he bore the wounds of the
Lord Jesus in his heart."

It was the sufferings of the Crucified One that stood before his
eyes, when as a young man he went and wept in the woods by
Portiuncula. A person met him there one day and asked the
reason of his sorrow. "I am weeping," answered Francis, for "the
pain of my Lord Jesus Christ!" And so great, so real was his
unhappiness, that even the other began to weep.

To honor the Cross was the object of the prayer Francis had
prescribed for his Brothers. "We pray to Thee, O Lord, and
praise Thee, because with Thy Holy Cross Thou hast redeemed
the world!" And he would never permit the Brothers to step

upon two straws or two twigs that were lying across each other.

And the others thought of him under the symbolism of the Cross. Silvester dreamt that a cross of gold went out of the mouth of Brother Francis and over the world, and Brother Pacificus saw him in a dream in the form of a cross pierced by two swords. Leo once saw a great gilded cross going in front of Francis.

In the Mass of the Feast of the Exaltation of the Holy Cross it is as if places in the Liturgy were given for all the words of the Church and gospel referring to the Cross. "This sign of the Cross," it says, "shall stand in heaven when the Lord comes to judgment." Or, in the words of Paul: "We should be glorified in the Cross of our Lord Jesus Christ, in whom is our salvation, life, and resurrection." Or the following: "Christ, our Savior, who saved Peter on the sea, save us, have mercy on us by the power of Thy Cross." "Thou strong Cross, thou noble Cross, nobler than all the trees, no woods produce thy equal, a tree with such leaves and flowers," is in a hymn for that day. And again about the Cross, to the Cross: "Thou art fairer than the cedars of Lebanon, thou art the tree of life in the middle of the garden of Paradise." "Behold the Cross of the Lord! Let all its enemies fly! The Lion of Judah's stem hath conquered, Alleluia!"

Penetrated by all these strong words, Francis lay in prayer outside his cell on the morning of the fourteenth of September. It was not yet day, but while awaiting the sunrise he prayed, with face turned to the east, with hands upraised and extended arms:

"O Lord Jesus Christ, two favors I beg of Thee before I die. The first is, that I may, as far as it is possible, feel in my soul and in my body the suffering which Thou, O gentle Jesus, sustained in Thy bitter passion. And the second favor is, that I, as far as it is possible, may receive into my heart that excessive charity by which Thou, the Son of God, was inflamed, and which actuated Thee willingly to suffer so much for us sinners."

"And as he long prayed thus," says the old story, "he felt a certainty that God would vouchsafe him these two things, and that it would be given him to receive both parts, so far as it was possible for a creature. And after he had received this promise, he began with great devotion to meditate on the sufferings of Christ and on the boundless charity of Christ, and the glow of piety grew so strong in him, that with charity and pity he was all transformed to Jesus.

"And as he lay in this prayer and burned with this flame, behold, it came to pass that he in the same morning hour saw a seraph coming down from heaven with six luminous wings. And the seraph slowly approached Francis, so that he could discern and clearly see that it bore an image of a crucified man, and its wings were so placed that two were raised over the head, two were extended for flight, and with two it covered its body.

"But when Francis saw this vision he was much frightened, and at the same time he was filled with joy and sorrow and wonder. For he had great joy in the gentle Jesus who showed Himself to him so intimately and looked so lovingly upon him, but it gave him inexpressible sorrow to see the Lord fastened to the Cross. And, moreover, he wondered over so unusual and astonishing a vision, for he knew that mortal suffering is not compatible with a seraph's immortal spirit. But as he wondered thus, it was revealed to him by the one before him that he should understand that it was not by bodily martyrdom, but through an inner flame, that he should be transformed entirely into the likeness of Christ the Crucified.

"But now after the wonderful vision had finally disappeared, an excessive glow was left in Francis' heart, and a living love of God, and in his body the vision left a wonderful image and imprint of Christ's sufferings. For at once in his hands and feet marks like nails began to appear, so that they seemed perforated in the middle, and the heads of the nails were within the palms of the hands and on the top of the feet, and the points of the nails were on the backs of the hands and under the feet, and they were bent over, so that there was space between the flesh and points of the nails for a finger, as if in a ring, and the nails had a round, black head. And so in his left side the image of a lance-thrust appeared, without cicatrix, but red and bleeding, out of which blood often issued from Brother Francis' breast and saturated his habit and clothes.

"But Francis said nothing of this to the Brothers, but hid his hands, and he could not put the soles of his feet to the earth anymore. And the Brothers found that his habit and clothes were bloody when they went to the wash, and then they understood that he bore the image and likeness of our Lord Jesus Christ the Crucified in his side and likewise on his hands and feet."

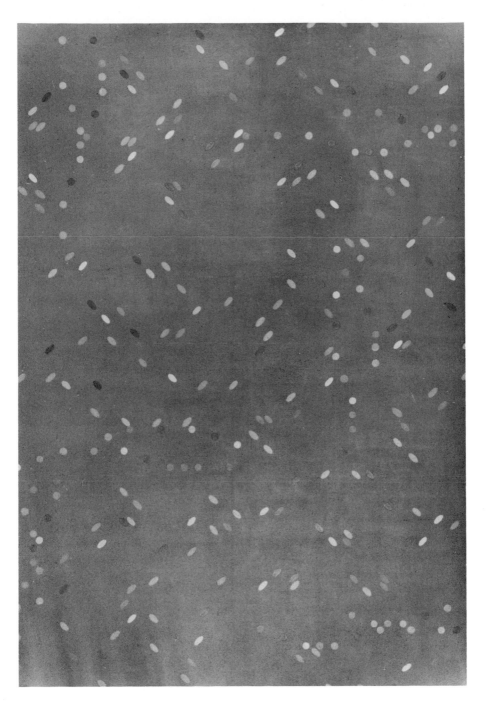

THE PRAYERS OF ST FRANCIS

"Mary Queen of Scots." Artist: Larry Poons. Courtesy of Mr. and Mrs. Robert C. Scull. Photograph by Eric Pollitzer.

PART SIX

The Prayers of Saint Francis

The Praises of the Most High

You alone are holy, Lord God, Worker of Wonders.
You are strong.
You are great.
You are the Most High.
You are omnipotent, Our Holy Father, Lord of heaven and earth.
You, Lord God, one and three, are our every good.
You, Lord God, are good, all good, our highest good—Lord God living and true.
You are charity and love.
You are wisdom.
You are humility.
You are patience.
You are a firm anchor.
You are peace.
You are joy and happiness.
You are justice and temperance.
You are the fullness of riches.
You are beauty.
You are gentleness.

An autograph copy of this prayer is conserved in Assisi to this day. The prayers in this part have been translated from the Latin by the editor.

You are our protector.
You are our guardian and defender.
You are our strength.
You are refreshment.
You are our great hope.
You are our faith.
You are our most profound sweetness.
You are our eternal life, great and admirable Lord, Omnipotent
    God.
Holy and merciful Savior!

The Blessing of Brother Leo

The Lord bless you and keep you:
The Lord make his face to shine upon you and be gracious to you:
The Lord lift up his countenance upon you and give you peace.
Brother Leo: The Lord bless you!

Conserved in autograph on the opposite side of the parchment containing "The Praises of the Most High." It consists of the patriarchal blessing for their children followed by the line "Brother Leo: The Lord bless you" to which Francis added a drawing of a skull and a cross.

The Praise of Virtue

I salute you, Regal Wisdom. May the Lord safeguard you with your holy sister, Unsullied Simplicity.

Holy Lady Poverty! May the Lord watch over you and your sister, Holy Humility.

My pious Lady Charity! May the Lord watch over you and your holy sister, Obedience.

May the Lord protect all of you holy virtues, for you find your source in him and come forth from him.

No man in this world can possess you if he does not die to self.

He who possesses one of you, without offending the others, possesses all.

He who offends one of you lacks all and offends against all.

Both a prayer and a poem in honor of virtue, it is unclear just when Saint Francis wrote it.

Each of you drives out vice and sin.

Holy Wisdom overcomes Satan and his wiles.

Holy and pure Simplicity confounds the wisdom of this world and
fleshly desires.

Holy Poverty drives out cupidity, avarice, and earthly desires.

Holy Humility overcomes pride, the men of this world, and all
terrestrial things.

Holy Charity confounds all temptations of the flesh and the devil
and all human fears.

Holy Obedience drives out carnal and bodily desires and keeps
the body in check.
    It holds us subject to the Spirit and obedient to our brothers.
    It keeps us submissive to all the men of the world, and not
    only to men, but to the animals and flowers, who can do what
    they want with us to the extent that God has given them
    power over us.

Prayer to the Blessed Virgin Mary

Mary, I salute you. You are our Holy Lady, Most Holy Queen, and Mother of God.

You are ever Virgin, elect of the Father, consecrated by him with his most holy beloved Son and the holy Paraclete.

In you is the fullness of grace and all good.

I salute you as the palace, tabernacle, and house of God.

I salute you, his garment;
                his handmaid;
                his Mother.

Accepted as authentic by almost all critics, the date of its composition has not been fully established by scholars.

The Prayer "Omnipotens"

Omnipotent, eternal, just, and most merciful God: grant us miserable sinners the grace to know your will and to do those things which please you. Thus, purified in our hearts and enlightened and illuminated by the fire of your Holy Spirit, we can follow in the footsteps of your Son and our Lord Jesus Christ and, through your grace, we may attain to him.

We ask this through you who are undivided Trinity and perfect unity living and reigning forever in the glory of Almighty God. Amen.

Some manuscripts place this prayer as part of a letter Saint Francis wrote to a general chapter of the brothers. There is still uncertainty as to its place and time of composition.

A Prayer of Praise and Thanksgiving

We thank you, Most High and holy God, righteous and holy Father, Lord of creation and King of the heavens, because through your holy will and your only Son and the Holy Spirit, you have created all things visible and invisible, and we, made in your image and likeness, were placed in paradise and through our fault are fallen. We further thank you through your Son, who created us and who loved you, and through that love was born true man and true God of the glorious and most holy Virgin Mary; we thank you that through the merits of his cross and his blood and death, we have been ransomed from slavery. We thank you because your Son will come again in the glory of his majesty to send evildoers who refuse to do penance to the eternal flames, while those who serve, adore, and confess you will hear, "Come, blessed of my Father, enter into the possession of the kingdom which has been prepared from the beginning of the world."

We miserable sinners are not worthy to call out your name, so we beseech our Lord Jesus Christ, your beloved Son, "in whom you are well pleased," to thank you himself in concert with the Holy Spirit, the Paraclete, to give thanks to you as it is pleasing to you and to them through whom you have done so much good

This long hymn of praise makes up the final chapter of the first rule of Saint Francis (1221) and has been slightly adapted.

for us. Alleluia. We praise in the name of your love, your glorious Mother, the most Blessed Virgin Mary, blessed Michael, Gabriel, and Raphael, together with all the choirs of the holy angels, seraphim, cherubim, thrones, dominations, powers, principalities, virtues, angels, archangels; likewise blessed John the Baptist, John the Evangelist, Peter, Paul, the blessed patriarchs, prophets, innocents, Apostles, evangelists, disciples, martyrs, confessors, virgins, Blessed Elias and Henoch, and all the saints who were, are, and will be. As it would be pleasing to them so for the all graces we have received, we render you thanks our highest and most holy God, eternal and living, together with our Lord Jesus Christ and the Holy Spirit, the Paraclete, forever and ever. Amen. Alleluia.

We, the least of the brethern, useless servants, humbly and insistently pray that everyone will persevere in the faith outside of which there is no salvation. We pray especially for those who are part of the patrimony of the Apostolic Catholic Church who desire to serve the Lord God: All the ecclesiastical orders, priests, deacons, subdeacons, acolytes, exorcists, lectors, porters, all clerics, all male and female religious, all children and infants, the poor and the rich, the kings and princes, workers, farmers, laborers and managers, all the virgins, widows, married folk, laymen and laywomen, children and infants, young and old, healthy and ill, small and grown, every race, tribe, nationality and tongue, every country, and every individual in the world present and future. We love all of these "with all our heart, soul, mind, strength, will, and forces"; with all our energy, with every feeling, with every interior stirring, with all our desires, we shall love the Lord God who has given us body, soul, and life and who has redeemed and saved us through his mercy and has given us miserable, poor, evil, fetid, and ungrateful sinners every sort of good.

We should desire nothing else, look for nothing else, or find other pleasure or love outside of God who is creator, redeemer, and savior, for he alone is perfect, the source of all good, our

supreme good; he alone is holy, sweet, just, true, upright, innocent, pure; it is in and through him alone that we find every
pardon, every grace, all glory, and praise that is given to the just
on earth and the blessed in heaven. Therefore nothing should
divide, separate, or cause us to stray from him. Everyone of us,
at every hour and at every instant and at every place should
believe with constancy, love, serve, praise, bless, glorify, exalt,
and honor the eternal and highest God, triune and one, the
Father, Son, and Holy Spirit, creator of all things, savior of those
who believe, trust, and love him, who is without beginning or
end. For he is immutable, invisible, inerrant, ineffable, incompre-
hensible, unscrutable, blessed, worthy of praise, glorious, exalted, sublime, amiable, loving, and, above all, the only one who
is worthy of desire in all eternity.

Glory be to the Father, to the Son, and to the Holy Spirit as
it was in the beginning, is now, and ever shall be.

Amen.

The Prayer of Saint Francis

Lord, make me an instrument of your peace.
Where there is hatred, let me sow love.
Where there is injury . . . pardon.
Where there is discord . . . unity.
Where there is doubt . . . faith.
Where there is error . . . truth.
Where there is despair . . . hope.
Where there is sadness . . . joy.
Where there is darkness . . . light.
    O Divine Master, grant that I may not so much seek
To be consoled . . . as to console.
To be understood . . . as to understand.
To be loved . . . as to love.
       For:
It is in giving . . . that we receive.
It is in pardoning, that we are pardoned.
It is in dying . . . that we are born to eternal life.
Amen.

This well-known prayer, often ascribed to Francis, was written by an unknown person in this century.

72 73 10 9 8 7 6 5 4 3 2 1